An Ancient Air

The invention all admired and each how he
To be the inventor missed; so easy it seemed
Once found, which yet unfound
Most would have thought impossible.

Milton

An Ancient Air

A Biography of John Stringfellow of Chard
The Victorian aeronautical pioneer

Harald Penrose

Smithsonian Institution Press
Washington, D.C.

Author of:-
I flew with the Birds
No Echo in the Sky
Airymouse
Cloud Cuckooland
British Aviation: The Pioneer Years
British Aviation: The Great War and Armistice
British Aviation: The Adventuring Years
British Aviation: Widening Horizons
British Aviation: The Ominous Skies
Wings Across the World
Adventure with Fate
Architect of Wings

Copyright © Harald Penrose 1989

First published in the United States 1989 by
Smithsonian Institution Press with the permission of
Airlife Publishing, England.

ISBN 0-87474-752-X

Library of Congress Catalog Number 88-060696

Printed in England.

Contents

Acknowledgements

Introducing some of the many who assisted

The route to a biography is long and tortuous and requires the help of many people. Years may elapse before sufficient clues are established to plot the course. Certainly in the case of John Stringfellow this has been a long term interest, but I did not undertake more extended research until discovering that Mrs Irene White, the daughter of his grandson Valentine Stringfellow, lived not far from my village and was a zealous protagonist of her great-grandfather's contribution to aeronautics, owned many of his possessions and had amassed considerable documentation that was concurrent with his lifetime. All was placed at my disposal.

Armed with this background knowledge, I began to explore more deeply than the late M J B Davy was able to do for his classic *Henson and Stringfellow* published in 1931 on behalf of the Science Museum, of which he was Keeper of the aircraft section. An early discovery was a collection of letters from Henson to Stringfellow held by the Somerset Archaeological and Natural History Society in their library at Taunton Castle, together with two boxes of Stringfellow's photographic portrait negatives.

More correspondence came to light in 1956 when A M Ballantyne and J Laurence Pritchard, at that time the respective current and former Secretaries of the Royal Aeronautical Society, gave a lecture to the Yeovil Branch on *The Lives and Work of William Samuel Henson and John Stringfellow* in which extracts were quoted from unpublished letters written by the Society's earliest Secretary, F W Brearey, to Stringfellow. Subsequently Pritchard, a friend since my student days, offered me the use of the originals, and more recently, through the good offices of Arnold Nayler, the RAeS Librarian, I was able to purchase from the Society photocopies of the full correspondence to incorporate in this biography.

However a large album of Stringfellow memorabilia I had noted in 1960 among other unguarded items in the vestibule of the Society's headquarters in London had apparently disappeared without trace by 1965; as had valuable historical reports quoted by J E Hodgson in his long ignored article *Henson's 'Aerial*

Steam Carriage' 1843 published in the Journal of the RAeS in April 1943 — yet timely coincidence through the kind co-operation of Brian Knight, chairman of Chard Museum, recently led to contact with J W Chapman, great-grandson of the renowned John Chapman who wrote those records, with the result that I was given photocopies of the drafts of a number of other originals revealing his connection with Henson.

John Bagley, Curator of the Aeronautical Collection of the Science Museum, sent prints of hitherto unknown significant correspondence between John Stringfellow and Chapman together with letters from Alderson to Frederick Stringfellow. Other correspondence from Alderson relating to the gift of Stringfellow models by Patrick Alexander to the Victoria and Albert Museum was discovered and copies sent to me by Gordon Cullingham, archivist to the Windsor History Group. Similarly Philip Jarrett sent fascinating 1843 press reports and magazine articles on Henson's proposed 'Aerial Steam Carriage'.

To the late 'Fitz' H F G Cowley I am indebted for the unique photographs of models and components he bought in August 1961 at an auction by Hodgson & Co, of books and albums from the estate of a J R Pike, though how he obtained them is not known. Unfortunately Fitz failed to realize the importance of the ensuing Lot 61 comprising eleven Stringfellow negatives 'including machines and a portrait', so did not buy them.

Many others have also contributed interesting facets, among whom Leslie Hayward a patents expert who lectured at Yeovil on Henson and Stringfellow, A E White when Town Clerk of Chard, and especially L W Hoskins of the Chard History Group who delved into Stringfellow's association with Chard civic affairs. Rare prints and photographs of old Chard were loaned by L V Preston. Helpful information came from Mrs M J Alderson, Louis Casey of the Smithsonian Institution, the late Dennis Dodds, Miss Edwards of Chard Museum, Mike Goodall, Jack Handle, Mrs F S Hann, J K Haviland of Virginia University, Donald Hill, James Hutson of Library of Congress, the late S Paul Johnson of the Smithsonian, W James, Jane Kenamore the archivist of Galveston USA, M Maxted the Devon area librarian, Frank Maxfield of Sheffield, Elizabeth Pease, Margaret Penrose and Sheffield Library, the late P W Petter, Thos G Rice of Galveston, F S Smith when RAeS Librarian, the late V B T Stringfellow and Mrs Watters the great-granddaughter of Alan Harrison Stringfellow. But necessarily, from beginning to end, the correspondence, visits, research, and deductions devolved on the author in this attempt to evoke the image of his local hero, John Stringfellow.

Foreword
By Peter W Brooks

John Stringfellow and William Samuel Henson undoubtedly made important contributions to early aviation history. There has, nevertheless, been debate for many years about the relative importance of their contributions, of which Henson's has hitherto been assumed the greater. A brief recapitulation of their story should help explain this, and at the same time point up the significance of the new information provided by Harald Penrose's book.

Controversy has revolved mainly around two claims made long ago for Stringfellow but challenged in more recent times by several writers.

The claims are that Stringfellow:
— in 1848, designed and made the first engine-driven model aeroplane (a monoplane) to make a free flight.
— in 1868, designed and made another steam-driven model (this time a triplane) which was capable of, but did not achieve, free flight.

Tied up with these claims has been the question of the value of the work of Henson and Stringfellow as a technical development. Both men, but particularly Stringfellow, made highly successful light, small, steam engines, suitable for the propulsion of model aeroplanes.

The generally accepted story has been that in about 1840 Henson produced — or adapted from others — a number of new ideas which in 1842 culminated in the well-known 'Aerial Steam Carriage' patent specification. This described a projected steam-driven monoplane with a wing span of no less than 150 feet. The laden weight was to be an unrealistically small 3000 lb. The design attracted greater worldwide interest than any previous aeronautical proposal. It foretold to a remarkable degree many of the features of the practical aeroplane which was to emerge sixty years later. The extent of Stringfellow's involvement in this project was not clear.

The full-size machine was never built. The project ended with the failure of the associated premature airline, the 'Aerial Transit Company'. However, in December 1843, Henson and Stringfellow signed an agreement to co-operate in their future aeronautical activities. They started in 1844 with a small spring-powered model which proved unsatisfactory and then proceeded with a large twenty-foot wing span model scaled down from the full-size 'Aerial'. This was probably completed in 1845 and eventually unsuccessfully tested out-of-doors in a field at Bala (or Bewley) Down near Chard in Somerset.

Subsequently Stringfellow, on his own initiative, built a swallow-winged model which he claimed took off from a sloping wire and made a level or slightly climbing flight which was ended only by the twenty-two yard length of the room. A later demonstration took place at the Cremorne Gardens in London where the forty-yard length of the tent was said to have permitted a longer flight. Meanwhile Henson had married and in April 1848 emigrated to the United States *just before* these historic events.

Until recently, a twenty-year hiatus in Stringfellow's aviation activities had been assumed, his enthusiasm being revived by the formation in 1866 of the Aeronautical Society of Great Britain (later granted the Royal Assent). Harald Penrose's researches show that this was not so and that Stringfellow maintained his interest in aviation far beyond the triplane exhibited at the 1868 Crystal Palace Exhibition, which was previously thought to have concluded his activities. Stringfellow also passed on his enthusiasm to his son, Frederick John Stringfellow, who completed a biplane commenced by his father, and also constructed several steam engines as well as a multi-plane.

This meticulously researched new work by Harald Penrose, a chartered aeronautical engineer and early Westland test pilot, is a most welcome addition to the literature available on early aviation pioneers.

Peter W Brooks
July 1988

A Chronology of Nineteenth Century Britain

1799   John Stringfellow born at Attercliff, near the rising town of Sheffield. The dawning of the age of steam.

1800   Bill passed for Union of Britain and Ireland.

1805   Naval Battle of Trafalgar annihilates the combined fleets of France and Spain and relieves England of the threat of invasion by Napoleon.
Coalition of England, Russia and Austria against France.

1808-14 Peninsular War in Portugal fought by Britain and France.

1814   Wellington invades France by crossing the Pyrenees and reaches Toulouse. Napoleon abdicates; end of war.

1816   Twenty-two years war with France is followed by forty years peace, initially marred by home riots, distress and discontent, due to heavy taxation, ban on corn imports and substitution of machinery for hand labour.

1820   George IV becomes King.

1827   John Stringfellow marries Hannah Keetch.

1829   Roman Catholic Relief Bill passed, giving freedom of worship. Sir Robert Peel establishes policemen in lieu of night watchmen.

1831   William IV, the 'sailor King', crowned. Stringfellow launches celebratory balloon at Chard, Somerset.

1832   Parliamentary Reform Bill passed extending voting rights. Stringfellow marks occasion with another balloon.

1833   Factory Act debars employment of children under nine and limits working hours of all women and young persons under eighteen to twelve hours a day.

1836   Marriage Act permitting Nonconformists to be married in their own chapels or before registrar.

1837   Princess Victoria succeeds as Queen.

1839-40   War in Afghanistan to prevent Russia making an alliance and invading India on her north-west frontier.

1840   Penny postage introduced, replacing the charge of four pence per half ounce.

Queen marries her cousin Prince Albert of Saxe-Coburg.

1841   China agrees to open five ports to British trade and cedes Hong Kong to Britain.

1842   Income Tax established.

W S Henson joins Stringfellow at Chard to build and experiment with a twenty-foot model of a monoplane patented by the former.

1843   Disruption in Church of Scotland results in the establishment of the Free Church of Scotland.

1845   The first Sikh War in India follows war with the Sindh.

Famine in Ireland.

1846   Nationwide agitation leads to the repeal of the Corn Laws.

1848   Henson emigrates to America after the failure of his huge model, but Stringfellow establishes the world's first powered, winged flight with a ten-foot model of his own design.

1849   Stringfellow and son Frederick John visit America, and the latter remains there to manage his maternal grandmother's business at Galveston.

1850   Bill passed giving representative government to four Australian colonies: New South Wales, Victoria, South Australia and Van Diemen's Land.

Constitution also granted to each of six New Zealand colonies.

1851   First of the world's great industrial exhibitions held in the specially built 'Crystal Palace' in Hyde Park, London.

1853   Stringfellow patents galvanic battery for medical use.

1854   War with Russia. Battle of Balaclava and famous charge of the Light Brigade.

1856   Peace established. Russia agrees concessions.

1857   Indian Mutiny put down after bitter fighting.

1858   British government ends authority of the East India Company by transferring its power to the Crown.

1859   Fear of French invasion leads to formation of Volunteer Corps as part of the regular army.

1861-5   American Civil War arising from contention between North and South on exploitation of slaves. War causes cotton shortage in England due to cessation of supplies from America.

1862-3   Frederick Stringfellow closes Galveston business due to advancing war and returns to England.

1866   Aeronautical Society of Great Britain founded.

1867   Second Parliamentary Reform Bill enacted.

Irish uprisings and outrages break out in hope of separating from England, but suppressed by Irish Constabulary with little bloodshed.

Dominion states under name of 'Canada' given to the North American Colonies.

1868   Aeronautical Society holds world's first aero-exhibition at Crystal Palace re-erected at Sydenham, London. Stringfellow demonstrates triplane model and wins prize for small steam engine.

1870   Irish Land Act passed giving compensation to outgoing tenants and establishing courts of arbitration.

Franco-Prussian War in which Germany joins Russia and invades France. Napoleon taken prisoner.

1871   Paris taken. Peace signed. Russia released from engagement forbidding warships in the Black Sea.

1877   Russo-Turkish War. Turkish army defeated. To prevent Russians occupying Constantinople the British fleet is ordered to sail to the Sea of Marmora.

1878   Treaty signed between Russia and Turkey but British insist document must be submitted to all European powers. As the Treaty of Berlin it results in the re-allocating of independencies of Balkan States and several territorial adjustments of which Cyprus is ceded to England.

1879   Egypt declared bankrupt and placed under dual control of France and England.

1882   Insurrection in Egypt, so England temporarily assumes protectorate.

1883   The followers of a Mohammedan fanatic, the Mahdi, destroy an Egyptian army of 11,000 men, and the Sudan is temporarily abandoned by the British.

John Stringfellow dies at Chard.

1885   General Gordon arrives in Khartoum, to negotiate the withdrawal of Egyptian troops from Sudan but is murdered. Khartoum remains in the hands of Kalifa and the Dervishes until 1898.

1886   Bill for Home Rule for Ireland defeated. Queen dissolves Parliament and the succeeding party of Conservatives and Liberal Unionists has a powerful majority.

1887   Celebration nationwide of Queen's Jubilee.

1890   Treaty between British, French, German, Portuguese and Italian governments defining 'spheres of influence' in Africa. Heligoland is ceded to Germany.

1893   Attempt to introduce Second Home Rule Bill for Ireland dismissed by House of Lords by an unprecedented 419 to 4 votes.

Parish Councils Bill for England completes process of local self-government begun with the Reform Act of 1832.

1896   In South Africa the Boer settlers refuse to grant electoral rights and privileges to influx of British and other nationalities attracted by discovery of gold and diamonds.

1898   Combined English and Egyptian forces under General Kitchener re-take the Sudan.

United States sends ultimatum to Spain demanding independence of Cuba. War ensues and Spanish fleet destroyed. Treaty follows by which Cuba is released from Spanish control and the Philippine Islands are ceded to USA.

1899   In South Africa President Kruger pursues idea of independence and absolute control of the whole country. War ensues. The Transvaal Boers invade Natal. Conflagration spreads and British army suffers reverses. Reinforcements sent from England, supported by volunteer troops from Canada, Australia and New Zealand.

Boers defeated after bitter fighting, and Britain formally annexes the Orange Free State.

1900   In September, by the Queen's Proclamation, the Commonwealth of Australia is announced, comprising New South Wales, South Australia, Western Australia, Queensland and Tasmania.

1901   Death of Queen Victoria after a reign of sixty-four years. Her eldest son Edward VII becomes King.

1905   Death of Frederick John Stringfellow.

A map of Britain showing important locations referred to in the text.

Chapter 1

Age of Industrial Development

At Westminster Abbey, amid pageantry and pomp, the clergy and massed nobility were crowning the royally-robed William IV, genial third son of George III. Every town and village in England was celebrating the occasion with joyous relief after the profligate and scandal-provoking ten-year reign of William's elder brother 'Prinny', King George IV. By contrast, William's accession a year before had been welcomed everywhere with acclamation. In his brother's reign he had been Lord High Admiral and now became popularly known as the 'Sailor King', for his character had all those qualities of a sea-going man that were so popular with the English, though at sixty-six he was rather old to become a monarch.

Great crowds thronged the precincts of Westminster. Within the Abbey a brilliant scene was set. Forty gentlemen dressed in blue frock-coats with crimson sashes, white breeches and stockings, each carrying a gilt staff, conducted the elegantly attired aristocracy and their bejewelled ladies to their proper places, and three-quarters of the Commons were arrayed in military uniforms. The horsedrawn equipages of the nobility were magnificent, and the royal carriage was drawn by eight horses, with four grooms each side, two footmen at each door, and a Yeoman of the Guard at each wheel. The vast crowd watching the arrivals was delighted at the pageantry and particularly pleased that at last they had a Queen to gaze upon.

For everyone everywhere the Coronation meant a national Gala day amid fluttering flags and bunting. At Chard, a prospering little Somerset borough town and parish, the wide main street, bordered either side with a narrow stream in which small boys loved to paddle, was thronged with excited men and women and children, for such celebrations were all too rare in the quietly toiling life of the countryside. Here were dancing and side-shows, booths selling ribbons and frills and good honest broadcloth, stalls with pots and pans, trestle tables of pies and cakes, and barrels of flowing ale and cider.

But there was even greater cause for excitement because it had been advertised that a celebratory 'Navigation of the Air' would be made by a hot-air balloon. They were still objects of wonder, though invented fifty years ago, but none had been seen at Chard until this great occasion. With tense anticipation the crowd watched the suspended big silk bag slowly distending after the naptha furnace at its open neck had been lit. Soon it became a magnificent many coloured orb glistening in the sunlight. As it rose there came a great gasp, then cheer upon cheer. Majestically the balloon lifted higher and higher above the long main street and skyline roofs of shops and houses, drifting eastward and growing smaller and smaller until it became a mere dot above the heights of Windwhistle hill, four miles distant.

That night Arthur Hull, a rising Parish Assistant Overseer who worked part-time on his father's farm near Chard, wrote in the diary he had kept since the age of twenty-four: '8 September 1831. King William IV crowned. Balloon let up, constructed by Mr Stringfellow, and it pitched at Windwhistle'. This is the first authenticated record proving that John Stringfellow was active in aeronautics a decade earlier than hitherto ascribed by historians — so his interest in such matters may well have started long before that.

At thirty-two he was an established specialist 'Bobbin and Bobbin Carriage' machinery maker in the extensive local lace trade and had been living at Chard for the preceding eleven years. Born on 6 December 1799 at a house near Townwell Yard in the growing village of Attercliff on the outskirts of a still rural Sheffield, he had been fascinated even as a youngster in watching his ingenious father, William Stringfellow, who was born in 1772, making mechanical contrivances of one kind and another — but he was a cutler by trade. He must have been outstanding, for the *Sheffield Iris* reported: 'His thoroughness for scientific experiments and mechanical pursuits induced him to erect near his residence, a small laboratory and workshop, which, from his rare talent and great ingenuity, was frequently resorted to by the lovers of science and mechanism. This little establishment was the first in this neighbourhood to be illuminated by gas. He found occupation for leisure hours in practising, as no mean adept, the various trades of gunsmith, locksmith, clockmaker, manufacturer of mechanical models, gas apparatus, philosophical instruments, and was well known in the neighbourhood as a skilful herbalist, botanist and florist.' His son John showed early sign of inheriting similar abilities.

Attercliff in those days took precedence over Sheffield, the name meaning 'village at the cliff' at a bend of the River Don, and in 1806 was described as having 'surroundings of rural beauty with scenery of hill and dale, of wood and water. Of most pleasing character, the flowing river is well stocked with a variety of fish, and on the banks of both sides are large magnificent trees. The village is studded with plantations and orchards, and fruit trees overhang the footpath in many parts of the main street.' Folk living in Sheffield would take a horsedrawn coach trip to Attercliff to visit the pleasure grounds as an ideal day's holiday for there was a cricket field, a race course, a bowling green and a maze. Contrasting with the several sequestered mansions and gardens with beautiful lawns were forges, a refinery, a foundry, a rolling mill and several timber mills on the village outskirts adjacent to the Rotherham and Doncaster highway. There was even a gibbet which still contained the bleached bones of a highwayman who was hanged eight years before John String- fellow was born and remained there for thirty years, thereafter said to have been ground into powder and mixed with clay at Swinton Pottery Works, giving rise to the name 'Bone China'!

John Stringfellow was born into a world of expanding scientific discoveries. Although horseback, the stagecoach, and the sailing ship were still the only means of long distance travel, the opening era of civil engineering had already begun in the reign of George III, aided by a ten-fold increase in the production of iron due to substitution of pit coal for the wood charcoal hitherto used. Introduction of reverberatory blast furnaces resulted in manufac- ture of rolled bar-iron and led to the first iron bridges with single arches of 100 feet or more, such as Telford's built to span the Severn in 1796.

Meanwhile, steam as a source of mechanical power was leading to extensive industrial development in this age of new creation. In 1769, Smeaton had greatly improved the steam engine that had been devised by Newcomen sixty years earlier, and in the form of a massive beam-crank engine was widely used in all parts of the kingdom to pump water from mines. Then in 1782 James Watt developed the engine to a pitch of perfection by incorporating a rotary motion to drive all kinds of machinery for such purposes as milling lumber, cotton spinning, corn grinding, or propelling ships and even carriages.

Nevertheless these were troubled times. Despite the decisive Battle of Trafalgar in 1805 there was continuing war, for France had invaded Portugal and the people of the Peninsular had risen against Napoleon — so young John Stringfellow at ten would have heard of the great heroes Sir John Moore and Sir Arthur Wellesley who became Viscount Wellington of Talavera in 1809. But the battles of the Peninsular war continued through the years until 1814 when the Treaty of Paris was signed between England, France, Russia, Austria and Prussia. Yet though imprisoned on the Isle of Elba, Napoleon escaped — only to be defeated the following year at Waterloo near Brussels.

Young John Stringfellow by then would have had at least a year as an apprentice to a bobbin-net lace manufacturer in Nottingham, to which city his parents had moved, as attested by G R Vine in his history, *Old Attercliff*.

Nottingham had long been famous for lace production, using warp machines that made a solid net web which could be cut without unravelling, but a new era was inaugurated in 1809 when John Heathcote patented a complex bobbin-net traversing machine which made it possible for an infinite number of threads to twist or wrap round each other and cause any one thread to traverse mesh by mesh all other threads in the width of the fabrication. It became the foundation of an extensive industry and the inventor reaped both honour and wealth for his ingenuity. Various inventive minds modified and improved his device, of which the most important was effected by John Levers in 1813, comprising a long cast-iron bed housing the mechanism, as well as anchoring the long, vertical warp frame handstrung with thousands of close-set threads from lower to top roller. Behind, corresponding to the interspaces, a weft-wide arrangement termed a comb-bar or bolt-bar held a long row of small, disc-like grooved bobbins 1½ mm thick supported in a tight-fitting, almost triangular 'bobbin carriage'.

With the first movement of the machinery each bobbin and thread passes through two of the vertical warp threads and lodges in a similar bolt-bar on the opposite side, which after receiving the bobbin with its forward motion, draws back, then *shags* to one side, goes forward taking the thread through the next two warps and lodges the bobbin on the first bolt-bar one thread-space onward. By these movements each bobbin-thread in the long line is twisted round one upright thread, then the bobbin shifts to pass through the next pair while the warp threads steadily wind from the lower roller to the upper.

Many of the operatives were women engaged on bobbin winding. Threading the brass bobbin was a tedious job allocated to boys, but warping, using a row of some 200 wooden bobbins with their threads converging into groups on drums and then wound off on a long roller which required heavy lifting, was a major task for men. As an apprentice of the Nottingham Lace Guild, John Stringfellow, after learning the process of sorting and winding the yarn and threading the metal bobbins, would be allocated to a skilled 'twist hand' operating a pair of the big traversing machines. As the Chard History Group records: 'They would set these machines up, untying a bundle of warp threads and lead them through various guides to the net roller, and when all were connected and properly tensioned, the warp was ready. The many bobbin carriages were then placed in their slots, and after checking them, the machine was set in motion through overhead belt gear driven by a water operated mill-wheel. Once it began working, the twist-hand had to watch intently and if a thread broke it must be repaired immediately. The day's work might end with a piece of lace 80 yards long and 3 yards wide which was then unrolled from the net roller and folded into a bundle.'

Stringfellow had inherited his father's mechanical genius and presently mastered the exceptionally skilled art of making the crucial little metal bobbins and special carriages with arced base serated with locating grooves. They required the utmost precision. Soon he became widely known as an outstanding 'Bobbin and Carriage maker'.

During his days at Nottingham it is probable that he came to know an up-and-coming lace maker named William Henson whose son, William Samuel, born in May 1812, was only a few years old. Young Stringfellow may also have heard of John Wheatley, the ambitious owner of another small lace-making mill in Nottingham, who moved his business to Chard, Somerset, possibly as a consequence of riots in 1816 by a group known as 'Luddites' whose violence was directed against all forms of machinery because they deemed this responsible for their miserable living conditions and unemployment. Their actions led to suspension of the Habeas Corpus Act after rioters flung a stone through the window of the Prince Regent's carriage, but failed to suppress the secret Republican societies and clubs intent on Parliamentary reform who were stirring up disaffection.

Little is known of John's time in Nottingham, but his interest in science may well have led to perusal of the *Mechanics Magazine* or even old copies of *Nicholsons Journal,* the 1809 volume of which had an article 'On Aerial Navigation' written by an enquiring 36 year-old Yorkshire baronet, George Cayley, who for the first time laid down the principles of heavier-than-air flight based on his observations of a stream of air acting upon a model wing held at different angles of attack. Though he did not precisely define the design of a flying machine, Cayley stated he had made a large unmanned glider with a square sail-like wing, and he recorded: 'It was beautiful to see this noble white bird sail majestically from the top of the hill to any given point on the plain below with perfect steadiness and safety, according to the set of the rudder.'

Even to contemporary scientists his ideas seemed too far-fetched. Every one from priest to ploughman ridiculed the idea that man might fly with wings like a bird. The only way accepted as possible, was by using one of these new fangled balloons which the French had invented 'in defiance of God'.

Could Cayley's account have inspired young John? Certainly there was a tradition in the next century among the Maxwell descendants of the Stringfellow family in Sheffield that in 1820: 'Mother's great uncle John flew down Brook Hill with the aid of kite wings.'

A surviving Registry Certificate shows that her father was Joseph Stringfellow, who as a 25 year-old had married this lady on 12 August 1872 at St Giles Church, Sheffield. Though the family legend is not strict evidence it may reinforce the conception of Stringfellow's early interest in matters aeronautic.

Chapter 2
Days of the Reform Bill

The Luddite riots continued in this new machine age of industrial development. In 1817 a big contingent of Manchester operatives, who became known as the 'Blanketeers' because they were conspicuously clad in blankets for night-time sleeping by the roadside, marched towards London to petition the Regent but were stopped on the way and dispersed. That was followed by insurrection in Derbyshire, and in 1819 there was the 'Peterloo massacre' when a vast concourse of artisans met in St. Peter's Field, Manchester, to listen to a popular agitator known as 'Orator Hunt'. Mounted yeomanry supported by the 15th Hussars were sent by the city's magistrates to effect his capture, and in a fearsome charge by the soldiers a number of people were crushed to death and many wounded. That led to legislation known as the Six Acts designed to suppress riots and seditious meetings with strong repressive measures. Because the Midlands were particularly vulnerable to attacks on factories, many businesses, including the lace manufacturers, decided to move into the quieter realms of the West Country. Chard was one of the few towns with factory space available because its own cloth-weaving manufacture had fallen into decline, so 20 year-old John Stringfellow was sent there by his employers to install bobbin-net lace-making machinery in what was probably the six storey mill of J B Coles taken over by that same John Wheatley who had led the way to Somerset and by 1821 would be fully established as J Wheatley & Co. Others followed, such as William Oram & Co in Mill Lane, and Cuff & Co at Perry Street hamlet, three miles south of Chard. Soon they were keeping John Stringfellow profitably busy as the only local bobbin and carriage maker; but he was also gleaning knowledge of steam engine operation from the steam beam machine powering the Holyrood Mill. At the time there were some 500 steam engines in Britain providing power for factories or the vital pumps for mines. They looked gigantic in their engine houses, but few were rated more than 40 horse-power.

Stringfellow had also begun to take an interest in politics because the general outcry was for a form of Parliament based on universal suffrage. Though regarded as a modest and kindly young man, he could hold his own in talking and debating on any intellectual subject and held deep religious views which were probably ingrained through having Quaker parents. Certainly he was sympathetic to the three important Labour Acts of 1824 which repealed the laws permitting magistrates to fix the wages of workmen, or prevented workmen from seeking employment by travelling to different parts of the country, but made combinations of masters and men legal for the purposes of fixing wages or conditions of work.

The next year saw a great crisis in Ireland because the Catholic Association had become so powerful that it almost superseded the Irish Government, but there was also great monetary panic in England caused by reckless speculations in wildcat Joint Stock companies, and sixty or seventy banks stopped payment, including Stuckey's at Chard — but the panic was checked by the Government 'influencing' the Bank of England to lend money to merchants upon security of their goods. However young Stringfellow was otherwise engrossed. He had met a beautiful local girl named Hannah Keetch, who was said to have been born in Newfoundland and certainly had relatives in Texas; where her parents are known to have lived in later years. The Chard Register shows they married on 24 February 1827, presumably in the Independent Baptist Chapel in East Street or the Second Baptist Fellowship in Holyrood Street, with Henry Selby, a gamekeeper, as witness. They settled in a house in Combe Street and at that time John must have been engaged in installing machinery in the rebuilt factory of Wheatley & Co which had been entirely destroyed by fire in the previous year, so was now being refurbished with the latest type of Levers bobbin-looms powered by a new type steam engine. John Riste, one of the company's skilled employees was made manager, and during the first year of restored operation, sufficient profit was earned to pay off the £40,000 loss caused by the fire. So prosperous had Chard become that in the year of Stringfellow's marriage there were forty-nine bobbin lace machines operating in Chard producing miles of wide plain netting in great demand for curtains, mosquito nets and trimming for ladies' hats and dresses. As recorded by the Chard History Group: 'There was a variety of these nets — Plain, Brussels, Chinese, Fancy or Thick Thread, as well as a little patterned lace for use on Jacquard machines which used punched paper to programme the desired pattern. There were also flounces and selveges.'

On 20 August 1828 Martha Ann, the first of the Stringfellows' children was born. William Henry followed on 12 September 1829. The third child, George, born on 6 July 1831, survived only a month as was all too often the case in those days of negligible medical knowledge. George's death was dutifully accepted amid the grief as 'the will of God'.

On 3 January of the following year, John Stringfellow's interest in ornithology and skill in taxidermy is indicated by Arthur Hull's diary entry: 'I carried a bittern to Mr Stringfellow to be stuffed.'

Like many another Reformist citizen of Chard, John was delighted when Parliament passed the Third Reform Bill, known as the Great Charter, which after much bye-play and coercion received the Royal Assent on 7 June 1832. Here was a great victory for the people, and for the first time the right of voting in Boroughs was given to all householders paying a yearly rental of £10, and in the Counties to freeholders to the value of 40s, copyholders to the value of £10 a year, and to long-term leaseholders who paid an annual rent of £50 and over. All the 'rotten boroughs' with less than 2,000 inhabitants were swept away, and thirty with less than 4,000 were deprived of one member. In the redistribution of seats the Counties were allocated 65 seats, and twenty-two large towns and the metropolitan districts were allowed two members each, with one member each for twenty-one smaller towns which had previously been unrepresented.

The triumphant Reformists and Freemen of Chard immediately set about organising a great Festival of Thanksgiving to be held on 20 July. The bells would be ringing, cannons fired, bands playing, banners flying and a great procession would march up Crimchard, 'turn wide as possible opposite Mr Wheadon's house; back up to the top of the Town; turn to the left opposite Mr Stringfellow's Shop; then out Holy-Rood Street, down Old Town, turn left within the Turnpike Gate up to the Market-Place and form in double Circles, with the Bands in the centre. The whole of the Bands will unite and play RULE BRITANNIA. Three CHEERS will be given for the KING and ROYAL FAMILY, and may they never forget the principles which placed them on the BRITISH THRONE.'

John and Hannah Stringfellow had further cause for jubilation. On 10 July their fourth child was born. The baptismal register of the Congregational Church of Chard enters his name as John; but from earliest years he was always known as Frederick John, or just Fred, to avoid confusion with his father, who at this juncture was completing yet another balloon which he would launch at the Festival in ten days time.

The *Chard and Ilminster Gazette* reported: 'Every day's nearer approach to Friday next increases the activity and bustle of preparation in this town, and the extensive scale of display has called forth the greatest alacrity, spirit, emulation, amongst all classes to render the great event as interesting as possible. Several hundred banners (many of which are of fine lace) are in preparation, to be embellished with various splendid devices and emblems and appropriate inscriptions, for which purpose all the painters in the town are busily employed. Ribbons in profusion are in demand from the haberdashers besides a numerous stock of other ornaments suited to the children who are to take the lead in the procession gaily attired and bearing small flags or baskets of flowers.

'A handsome appendage to the various other adornments to be worn on the occasion is the new medal of the Chard Political Union. This medal exhibits the Temple of Liberty, surmounted by Britannia, and at the entrance stands the roused Lion. On the three pillars are inscribed *Magna Charter, Bill of Rights, Reform Bill.*

'The day previous to the Festival is to be devoted by the Committee to the superintendence of the bread, beef, and beer distribution, of which one pound of the two former and one pint of the latter will be given to each of about three thousand individuals within the limits of the several Toll-Gates of the Town.'

Flamboyantly phrased posters at key points in town and villages gave the programme in full, with the marching orders, and an instruction that after the morning's marches and the cheers for King, Country, Reform, and Chard: 'All will disperse to their homes; the working classes to dine on the Provisions distributed the day before, the members of the Union and other Friends will dine at the GEORGE INN or else in the MARKET HOUSE.'

To the excitement of all who witnessed Stringfellow's Coronation balloon of the previous year, the Poster concluded with the announcement: 'The People will assemble again at Five o'clock in the Market Place to witness the Ascent of a SPLENDID BALLOON prepared by Messrs STRINGFELLOW, GARE and GARE.'

After that: 'At 7 o'clock BEER will be given away to be drank at the CORN-HILL.' But there was the injunction: 'At Ten o'clock it is expected that all fireworks and firing shall cease, and the people shall return to their homes in peace, rejoicing in the REFORM FESTIVAL held in CHARD, July 20th 1832.'

Of the Stringfellow balloon, no details have been discovered other than that 'Mrs Winter's mother stitched the silk for the balloon panels.'

The first elections under the Reform Bill followed early in 1833, with the Whigs greatly in the majority compared with the Royalist Tories who now assumed the name 'Conservatives', and the Whigs became known as 'Liberals', to whom for the rest of his days John Stringfellow remained a devoted member. Meanwhile his engineering business had so prospered that not only did he commission a Bath artist to paint splendid individual portraits of his wife and himself but also he was able to purchase three terraced houses on Snowdon Hill at the top of the town as well as the meadow of Field Bars behind them, with entrance road at the side of the end house to which he moved the family and added a workshop.

Shortly afterwards he was elected to the Chard Council and in 1834 became involved in administering the newly introduced Poor Law, which was designed to ameliorate the evils of pauperism. It enacted that parishes must unite into Unions with workhouses for those unable to keep themselves, but rigorously excluded out-door relief for the able-bodied. Stringfellow's experience of local factories in connection with their machinery was also of value to the Council in ensuring compliance with the new Factory Act which made it illegal to employ children under nine years old, and laid down that those under thirteen must not labour more than 8 hours a day, nor women and young persons under eighteen be employed more than 12 hours a day.

The same year also saw the establishment of the Chard Canal Company. With increasing production of Chard's wool and lace-mills the need for cheap bulk transport had long become evident. The cost of utilizing turnpike roads was high, but with steam-power replacing water-power for industrial use came increasing demand for South Wales coal. A canal link from Chard via Ilminster to the Taunton and Bridgwater Canal therefore seemed a hopeful solution to give direct access to the Severn estuary and promised increased local employment because a great lake-like water reservoir would have to be dug on the north-east side of Chard.

That September the Stringfellows' short-lived son Thomas George II was born, but fated to live only eighteen months.

*   *   *

The report of the Royal Commission on Municipal Corpora-tions in 1835 reveals that Chard was entitled to a Corporation of twelve burgesses of whom one was a Portreeve acting as annual Chairman elected at a meeting of the burgesses, each of whom generally held office in rotation as the duty was honorary. The officials comprised the town clerk appointed for life at 10 guineas yearly; a constable and two bailiffs who were unpaid; and a Town Crier who acted as beadle for which he received a new coat and hat on occasion. There was also an official churchwarden elected each year in the week preceding Easter. Under the new Act the head of the Corporation was styled 'Mayor' and under his leadership it was decided to build a new Corn Exchange at the centre of the High Street to replace the somewhat derelict Market House and Guild Hall.

In June, work started on the Chard Canal. It was slow, hard labour using pickaxes, shovels, and carts. Three tunnels had to be dug, and inclines cut at four places where the envisaged 28 foot tub barges would be floated onto carriages and dragged by horse over small hills. Keenly interested in the engineering and geological aspects, John Stringfellow paid a number of visits to various sections in the ensuing years and collected numerous fossils, several of which are still treasured by his great-grand-daughter.

He had many other devotions. Horticulture was one, and to that end he had built a conservatory at the back of his house with shelves of flowers and a grapevine growing on the southern wall — and it was still there a hundred years later. Hull's diary for 1 March 1835 indicates another facet with: 'I at Mr Stringfellow's this eve. Saw many experiments on the microscope.' In fact every mechanical and scientific development of those days fascinated him whether steam engines, the science of electricity, or the possibility of aerial flight.

The Rt Hon Margaret Bondfield PC, the first British woman Cabinet Minister, writing of her lace designer father William Bondfield in her biography *A Life's Work*, said: 'About 1835 John Stringfellow and William Henson, both in the lace trade, started experiments for making flying machines. Father often joined them, and with his own long-barrelled, muzzle-loading duck gun, shot all kinds of birds; these were weighed, measured and their flight tabulated, but no law or line could be found as to shape and size of wing from the flight of birds so they endeavoured to make moveable wings of various designs.'

That must have entailed free flight with hand-launched models, but no record survives as the day of photography had not yet dawned.

William Henson senior was thirteen years older than Stringfellow and though it is possible they had known each other from the time of John's apprenticeship in Nottingham, he had moved to Worcester by 1820 and then to Chard in the early 1830s. Described as an inventive genius in connection with lace making and knitting machinery, he had been granted several patents between 1825 and 1832 for small improvements on existing designs and methods of manufacture and more would follow.

Unfortunately Margaret Bondfield's references are ambiguous, for it is not clear whether she was referring to the elder Henson senior or his talented son William Samuel who was now 23 and regarded 36 year-old Stringfellow with dutiful respect as his senior but was already operating his own business of 'W S Henson, Lace Manufacturer, Chard'. Such was his mechanical aptitude that in October 1835, styled as 'machinist of Chard,' he obtained patent (No 68987) for improvements to machinery used by his father for manufacture of ornamental bobbin-net lace. Probably Margaret Bondfield meant the father, for his son never signed himself William but always with both Christian names or initials. Inevitably young Henson would become interested not only in his father's machinery developments but also in those experiments 'with moving wings of various designs'. He had an aspiring and inventive mind complementary to the much older Stringfellow's wide experience of bird flight and steam engine design, yet the relationship throughout their acquaintance seemed to remain that of master and acolyte. None of his many letters show any trace of familiarity for he always addressed Stringfellow as 'Dear Sir', and signed himself 'Very faithfully Yours'.

Stringfellow's Town Council duties were increasing. The Municipal Corporation Act of 1835 had restored to the inhabitants of towns the rights of self government of which they had been deprived since the 14th century. Election to the Council was no sinecure. Not only had education come to the fore but the Poor Law Act was necessitating re-establishment of local taxation, known as the 'Poor Rate', for which Stringfellow, as a highly respected person 'with estate exceeding £500', was elected 'Assessor' on 12 May 1836.

Stella, his second daughter, was born on 3 January of the following year and nine year-old Martha Ann was delighted to mother a small sister, though the young boys rather disdained her and were much more interested in the mechanical toys and small balloons that their father made for them.

Strict discipline was the keynote of bringing up all families and prayers were the regular prelude to breakfast. On Sundays the entire populace attended Church or Chapel twice a day. The children were not permitted playthings between the services and had to sit quietly reading the Bible and such improving books as *Pilgrim's Progress*. 'Sunday, the so called day of rest, was the most unpleasant of the week,' wrote a later contemporary of Stringfellow. 'We had no sort of recreation. Even walking except to Church, was forbidden. I have no doubt it was intended for our good, but I never in my youth had any agreeable recollection of the Sabbath day.'

John and Hannah were both intensely religious — so much so that on 23 March 1837 he was elected Borough Churchwarden responsible for the temporal affairs of the Church in conjunction with the Churchwarden annually elected by the Parish, but this caused consternation in Chard Town Council and John Langdon the Mayor, with three councillors, resigned because Stringfellow, as a member of the Independent Chapel, was regarded as a dissenter even though he had sworn the customary declaration that: 'I will never use my power by virtue as a Councillor to weaken the Protestant Church as by Law established in England.' His proposer, Alderman Cuff, took over as Deputy Mayor and must have smoothed ruffled feelings because ten days later Langdon returned as Mayor, the Churchwarden appointment having meanwhile been 'deemed illegal' despite the Bishop's decision that it was in order.

Chapter 3

Scheming a Powered Flyer

William IV, after a brief enfeebling illness, died on 20 June 1837, sincerely lamented for his kindness of heart and the simplicity of character that had endeared him to all classes of people. Nevertheless, the accession of the eighteen year-old Princess Victoria, and the novelty of a female Sovereign had charm for all, and when exactly a week after the burial of the King she went in State to meet Parliament she was received all along the line of the Procession with extraordinary enthusiasm. A tone of kindness, mercy and conciliaton befitting her youth and sex marked her first Speech from the Throne.

That autumn Stringfellow had the satisfaction of re-election as a Councillor. Though he tended to avoid contention and rarely attended meetings at the Chard Political Union, he sympathised with the country-wide outcry for a 'People's Charter', demanding six sweeping reforms comprising a vote to every man; voting by ballot; Parliament to be elected each year; the country divided into equal electoral districts; eligibility for Parliamentary membership to be regardless of property ownership; MPs to be unpaid — but in 1839 a petition signed by so called 'Chartist' delegates from all the large towns was rejected by Parliament. Riots followed, and agitation persisted for the next decade. Nevertheless the young Queen's Coronation on 28 June 1838 was celebrated in all the towns and villages to echo the great ceremony in Westminster Abbey, but there was no air balloon for Chard this time as Stringfellow was much engaged in more serious matters to sustain his growing family, which ultimately became six surviving boys and four girls.

Meanwhile he and a group of kindred thinkers formed the Chard Institution for the purpose of providing weekly lectures on a wide range of interests, excluding religion and politics. Arthur Hull the diarist recorded: '4 Jan. 1839. I at Chard. Saw Mr Stringfellow lecture on electricity, being the first time.' And in the following year: '17 January 1840. I at Mr Stringfellow's lecture eve, on electricity.' All the demonstration apparatus was made by Stringfellow. These and his later disquisitions were fluently written, revealing his philosophy, clarity of thought and extensive scientific investigations, but none dealt with aeronautics, even though the possibility of mechanical flight held such special charm for him. As Margaret Bondfield reported: 'On one occasion, when my father was present, Stringfellow took a square piece of cardboard and shot it across the room. "There!" he said, "Any surface will hold the air with applied power". From then on many ideas and experiments would lead to a wonderful little machine, embracing the new principles of screw-propeller, tubular boiler, and multiple planes.'

There was all too little time for devotion to that interest, but Henson's son William Samuel, now 27, had proved an apt pupil and was tackling the subject with scientific acumen. Adapting the comment that his mentor had made, he said: 'If any light and flat, or nearly flat, article be projected edgeways in a slightly inclined position, it will rise on the air till the force exerted is expanded, when the article will descend; and it will readily be conceived that if the article possessed a continuous power equal to that used in projecting it, the article would continue to ascend so long as the full part of the surface was upwards in respect to its hindpart. Such article if the power was stopped and the inclination reversed would descend by gravity, or by gravity aided by the force of the power if the power continued, thus imitating the flight of a bird.'

The two men must have had many an absorbing discussion on the possibilities of mechanical flight using fixed wings rather than 'wafting' them like a bird in the manner proposed by Sir George Cayley, who was now sixty-seven and currently endeavouring to form a 'Society for extending the application and improving the art of Aerial Navigation to be entitled *The Royal Aerostatic Institution'*, for he considered that steerable balloons with elongated envelope would be the practical solution long before mechanical winged flight became feasible. However his efforts to initiate the Society failed, despite much publicity by Charles Green, the most eminent aeronaut of the day, who hopefully proposed flying the Atlantic using a hand-driven propeller for his balloon. Even the idea of a marine screw-propeller was still novel, for it was only four years earlier that S P Smith, an Englishman, and John Ericsson, an American-Swede, had separately tried one for the propulsion of small ships instead of paddle wheels.

Reporting on Green's proposal, the *Mirror* of 4 April 1840 announced: 'To convince the scientific public in the practicability of his propelling or directing his balloon, causing it to ascend and descend without discharging gas or ballast, and in a tranquil atmosphere to move horizontally in any direction, Mr Green has commenced a series of important experiments at the Polytechnic Institution.'

A pair of oil portraits
thought to show John and
Hannah Stringfellow.

An early engraving of a hillside view of Chard showing the Windwhistle horizon

An early print of the Attercliff countryside showing the Arrow Inn.

Sir George Cayley, the reputed father of aerial navigation.

A painting of Chard *circa* 1830, showing the Guildhall blocking the High Street.

John Stringfellow in the early 1830s.

The Old Guildhall in the centre of Chard which was soon to be demolished.

The New Corn Exchange and Guildhall in Chard High Street *circa* 1860.

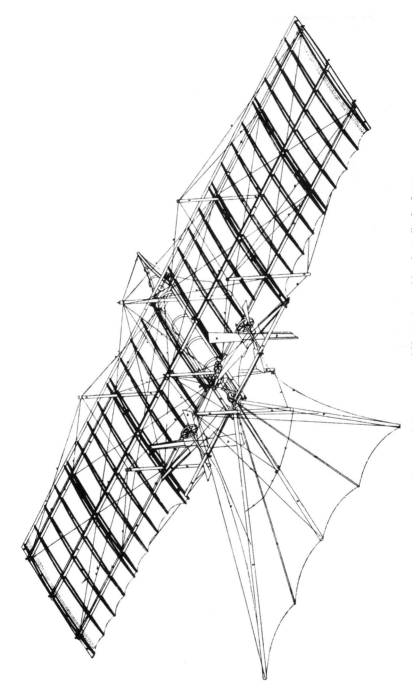

A patent drawing of the structure of Henson's machine foretells the future.

One of Stringfellow's small
industrial steam engines.

A Cruikshank caricature of
Henson's project.

THE HEIGHT OF SPECULATION—Groundless Expectations

John Stringfellow in middle age.

The restored Henson-Stringfellow Ariel model of 1844-47.

That eminent place of learning in Regent Street had been founded by Sir George Cayley two years earlier in order to show the public by practical demonstration 'the sound and important principles on which every science is based'. However, he had not actively pursued the subject of aeronautics for the past twenty years, nor had he or anyone else attempted any form of powered heavier-than-air flying despite the big, kite like glider he had launched unmanned in 1809. The fixed wings with which Stringfellow and Henson were experimenting were very different, based on the birds they had so industriously measured, and they were correct in their deduction that relatively long span was far more efficient than the more or less square wing used by Sir George Cayley. Certainly they were the first in the world to envisage and put into practice the idea of a steam engine driving twin multi-blade screw-propellers as tractive effort for a heavier-than-air machine. By giving them opposite rotation they also eliminated the turning and torque effect that a single propeller would induce, which in itself was a pioneering deduction, possibly from observation of those small, horizontally whirling, vertical lifting, fan-like propellers that were commonplace as toys. But developing a big one for horizontal propulsion would require much experimenting using a model steam engine and model propellers to glean an indication of the thrust.

The idea of making a man-carrying powered flier began to enthral them. According to their later chronicler Frederick W Brearey, one evening in 1840, the year of the Queen's marriage to her cousin Prince Albert of Saxe-Coburg, the two men met at Stringfellow's house and schemed a great aeroplane, putting into effect the experience gained with the model wings described by Bondfield's daughter. How far the joint design progressed in the ensuing months is not known, but eventually Henson departed to London, probably joining his father's business, for the *County of Somerset Directory* of 1840, published by W Bragg of Taunton, does not list him among the bobbin-net manufacturers at Chard, though Stringfellow features as the sole Bobbin and Carriage Maker. But perhaps the venture into powered flight was also taking too much of the latter's time as he was late for Council Meetings on several occasions and consequently subject to a fine of 2s 6d; so on 2 March he had seconded a motion that fines should be abolished, though to his irritation the vote was lost. However at that same meeting it was agreed that if Mr Stringfellow apprehended one Robert Mills and brought him in custody to Chard he should be indemnified by the Council for the arrears due of £34-4s-5¼d for the lighting rate collected by the said Robert Mills.

Chard was flourishing. The population at the last census was 5,141. Fore Street had been transformed by removing the unsightly Shambles slaughter house, Town Hall and Market House which had obstructed the centre, and an elegant combined Guildhall and Market House of Bath stone had been built parallel with the other houses. The convivial spirit of Chard was attested by 24 inns, and full employment accounted for by the five busy lace factories, numerous shopkeepers, saddle makers, straw-bonnet weavers, milliners and dressmakers, the two dozen hairdressers, fourteen tailors and nine shoemakers.

*   *   *

Henson was now living at Allen Street, Lambeth and apparently was 'experimenting with gliding models, constructional devices, and a light steam engine', the latter featuring a complicated valve and a condenser system intended to save water. Advising him in drawing up the specification for its proposed patent was a remarkable business acquaintance of his father's, John Chapman, a brilliant and cultured man of almost Stringfellow's age whose Loughborough lace-machine engineering business had failed in 1834 owing to the rigorous export protection laws. Chapman next moved to London, became craftsman to an instrument maker, then a tutor in mathematics, and subsequently wrote reviews of engineering developments for Joseph Clinton Robertson, the editor-owner of the *Mechanics Magazine* whose legal knowledge assisted many an inventor to secure a patent, among them Chapman himself who in 1836 devised an improved two-wheel version of Joseph Hansom's 'Safety Cab' by locating the coachman behind the fulcrum of the axle as counterpoise to relieve the deadweight load on the horse. A promotional company was formed, of which J C Robertson was one of the directors with Chapman as manager, and the patented Hansom became widely adopted all over Europe — but after three years Chapman was manoeuvred out of the business. In 1840 he was assistant editor of the *Mechanics Magazine* as well as helping the management of several other technical magazines, contributing to London newspapers, and also conducting a Patent Agency.

One of his clients was William Henson senior, still in the textile trade, who in November that year applied for a Patent (No 8708) for a knitting machine which was being financed by a John Duncan who was partner in a firm of solicitors and gave Chapman the task of hiring a workshop and organizing production. In turn this led to Henson's son William Samuel seeking Chapman's help in 1840 to draw up the specification for his 'improvements in steam engines', and Provisional Patent 8849 was granted for it on

16 February of the following year. Letters are extant in which Duncan urges haste to meet the deadline for filing in August. Even more significantly on 4 June that year Chapman sent him the calculations of steam power for the proposed Aerial Carriage which Duncan was probably proposing to finance.

That Henson's original inspirer John Stringfellow was already well-known for his own miniature steam engines is indicated by a paragraph in the local Chard newspaper of June 1841 headed 'Steam Engine by Post', stating that: 'Among odd things which have been sent through the Post Office since the recent introduction of the Penny postage rule a steam engine seems the most singular and unlikely article to be transmitted by letter. One was however posted at Chard for Stroud a few days ago, and has no doubt ere this safely reached its destination. It weighed with its package only 12 ounces, and was an exquisitely finished model constructed by our clever townsman, Mr Stringfellow, and kindly lent by him for an exhibition of a Scientific society at Stroud.'

That same month the newly fledged Great Western Railway completed its imposing seven-foot wide track from London to Bristol. John Stringfellow with his strong interest in steam engines undoubtedly would have taken coach to Bristol's newly opened, magnificent Temple Meads station to gaze in admiration at Brunel's cableless, hissing locomotives belching smoke from their tall chimneys, and ponder speculatively at the massive steam cylinders and huge pair of driving wheels. Later that year, probably when cut-price travel was initiated with an 'Express' drawn by two engines which reduced the original nine hour journey to Paddington to five hours forty-five minutes for a return fare of 21s, he went to London to visit the studiously eager Henson junior now twenty-nine years old. Perhaps it was on this journey that according to his later confidant F W Brearey: 'Mr Stringfellow in his efforts to determine the amount of supporting surface to sustain a given weight on some well ascertained basis, first availed himself of the Express train, by taking an arrangement for testing the resistance of aerofoils at various angles against the air at high speed.'

So special a visit must have been to discuss the drawings of the man-carrying cabin monoplane which Henson was formulating as the result of their earlier discussion. There is no evidence that he knew enough mathematics to calculate the strength of its wing spars and wire bracing system, but as John Chapman was so closely involved with him over the engine patent he was the likely man to undertake this task, though would not advertise the fact lest people thought him mad to be associated with so preposterous an idea as an engine-driven flying machine. Nevertheless at least he later guardedly admitted: 'My engagements up to 1842 were all connected with engineering subjects . . . I was called upon to prosecute research requiring more accurate and extensive knowledge of the resistance of the air than any former experiments had afforded.' Could it be that he was the actual designer of Henson's machine?

On 3 October of that significant year, Henson wrote to Chapman: 'Will you be good enough to let Mr Duncan have your report tomorrow morning as he insisted to have it as soon as possible? I shall be at Mr D's in the morning.' As the engine matters had been settled the report almost certainly referred to the flying machine.

A further purpose of Stringfellow's visit was to bring a small steam engine typical of those he constructed for use in the Chard lace mills. Consequently on 10 January 1842 Henson wrote from 7 Ralph Place, Trinity Square, London, apologising at not writing earlier because: 'I waited to give you some more particulars respecting my engine. The boiler consists of two cones 4½ ins dia. and 7 ins deep. The cones are like the tin I showed you at the time, having the upper part large enough to hold one of the cylinders above the waterline at the wide part.

'I find your cylinders will hold three times the quantity that mine will hold and consequently there should be something more than double the quantity of heating surface, but it will be advisable not to have double the weight of water. One quart of water is about the proper quantity for your boiler. It won't last long it is true, but that does not matter. My engine is heavier considerably than it ought to be, in addition to which it holds more water than is necessary. This is against me but still it is very powerful for its weight and I have no doubt about making it act. I have not yet got my model sufficiently advanced to 'have a fly' but I continue as sanguine as ever as to the result.'

He then refers to Stringfellow's participation, saying: 'I think you had better make the boiler of *several* small cones to get about 2½ times the surface with the same quantity of water — say 6 or 8 cones 2 or 3 ins dia. at the broad part, well studded with copper wire. My engine with water and fuel together with the fireplace weighs about 10 lbs but I am quite sure that an engine may be made of double the power with the same weight including everything and I know also that you can do it and will. I much wish I could have had your engine for my present model as it would assist so much in making up for those natural defects which all models possess more or less. Wishing you success, I am my dear Sir, very faithfully yours, W S Henson.'

Stringfellow appeared to have considerable specialised work from other quarters. Thus in the early 1840s he constructed a boiler which his son Frederick later said was 'for a common Steam Carriage' and in a vague reference to Henson mentions 'A similar one was patented in 1842 although it never worked.'

The next letter from 7 Ralph Place was dated 20 July 1842 and reveals a new aspect of the inventive Stringfellow as well as introducing Frederick Marriott, an ambitious and energetic Chard newspaper man and publicity agent, of whom Henson reports: 'Since you left here Mr Marriott called upon Weisse's and gave them to understand that he did not like the manner in which they received you. He told them also that you were quite as independent as themselves. In the course of conversation he gleaned that they were anxious about your Scarificater and he thinks that it would be to your advantage if by a little management they were induced to patent it. Weisse told him that he had sent an order of 200 Scarificaters to China about 3 weeks ago. I have no doubt that if you can by any means arrange matters with him it would be better than any other course as it would not be to their advantage under those circumstances to avoid the Patent in any way, but on the contrary they would defend the Patent from infringement and introduce the instrument all over the world simultaneously by means of their present extensive connection, thereby ensuring a good return in a short time and save you from an immense deal of anxiety and trouble. Weisse promised to send a letter to him for you proposing some terms, and I delayed writing on that account but they have not done so and I thought it better to write you the position so that you may judge for yourself how to proceed. I thought that part relating to the Scarificaters for China was worth knowing. I hope your father and mother are quite well also yourself. I shall daily expect to see you again in town.'

The so called 'Scarificater' was a surgical instrument Stringfellow had devised in the form of a blood-cupping device with lancet-pointed knife which had a 'stop' to prevent too deep an incision. They commanded extensive use because 'blood letting' in those and earlier days was regarded as essential action for every kind of disease.

A further indication of his wide ranging acceptance as a man of scientific knowledge was his appointment on 9 November to the Street Lighting Committee of Chard, linked with the associated production of coal gas for that purpose. Sadly, John's equally inventive father died at the end of that month.

Meanwhile on 29 September, Henson applied for a Provisional patent for his proposed steam-powered aeroplane described as 'Locomotive Apparatus for Air, Land and Water'. His address was given as 26 New City Chambers, Bishopsgate, probably the office of John Duncan. The specification did not claim the invention of an aeroplane but only 'certain improvements in locomotive apparatus and machinery for conveying letters, goods and passengers from place to place through the air', and adds that 'part of which improvements are applicable to locomotive and other machinery to be used on water or on land'. This could only refer to the steam boiler and not the power plant which he merely indicates 'as the best construction of steam engine I am acquainted with for the purpose of giving motion to suitable propellers' and is clearly of Stringfellow's derivation.

*   *   *

No sooner had the provisional patent been granted than Frederick Marriott and Henson, with the aid of D E Colombine, an attorney, agreed on a grandiose scheme to form the *Aerial Transit Company*, and a flamboyant PROPOSAL was published with intention of securing capital for the machine's construction. Apparently John Duncan had become bankrupt, so new backers were essential.

With fulsome and alluring phraseology the prospectus stated: 'An Invention has recently been discovered, which if ultimately successful will be without parallel even in the age which introduced the world to the wonderful effects of gas and of steam. This work, the result of years of labour and study, presents a wonderful instance of the adaptation of laws long since proved to the scientific world, combined with established principles so judiciously and carefully arranged as to produce a discovery perfect in all its parts and alike in harmony with the laws of nature and of science. The Invention has been subjected to several tests and examinations and the results are most satisfactory, so much so that nothing but the completion of the undertaking is required to determine its practical operation, which being once established, its utility is undoubted, as it would be a necessary possession of every Empire, and it is hardly too much to say of every individual of competent means in the civilised world . . .

'Patents will be immediately obtained in every country where protection to the first discoveries of an Invention is granted, and by the time these are perfected, which is estimated will be in the month of February 1843, the invention will be fit for Public Trial. Under these circumstance in furtherance of the Projector's views it is proposed to raise an immediate sum of £2,000 in 20 sums of £100 each (of which any subscriber may take one or more not exceeding five in number) the amount of which is to be paid into the hands of Mr Colombine as General Manager to be by him appropriated in procuring the several Patents and providing the expenses incidental to the work in progress. For each of which sums of £100 it is intended and agreed that 12 months after 1 February next, the several parties subscribing should receive as an equivalent for the risk to be run the sum of £300 provided that when the time arrives the Patent shall be found to answer the purposes intended.

'As full and complete success is alone looked to, no imperfect benefit is to be anticipated, but the work, if it once passes the necessary ordeal to which inventions of every kind must first be subject, will then be regarded by everyone as the most astonishing discovery of modern times. The intention is to work and prove the Patent by collective instead of individual aid as less hazardous and more advantageous in the result for the Inventor, as well as for others, by having the interest of several engaged in aiding one common object — the development of a Great Plan . . .

'It is not pretended to conceal the prospect is a speculation — all parties believe that perfect success, and thence incalculable advantages of every kind, will follow to every individual joining in this great undertaking; but the Gentlemen engaged in it wish that no concealment of the consequences, perfect success, or possible failure, shall in the slightest degree be inferred. They believe this will prove the germ of a mighty work, and in that belief call for the operation of others with no visionary object but a legitimate one before them to attain that point where perfect success will be secured from their combined exertions. All applications to be made to D. E. Colombine Esquire, 8, Carlton Chambers, Regent Street.'

Colombine was a well established lawyer friend of Marriott, and was able to induce a fellow attorney, 42 year-old John Arthur Roebuck, the MP for Bath and newly appointed as a QC, to procure the necessary incorporation of the company under Act of Parliament. Accordingly in January 1843 he presented a petition to the Commons for leave to bring in a Bill 'to authorise the transfer to more than 12 persons of a certain Patent granted to W. S. Henson'. The petition was duly referred to the Select Committee on Petitions for Private Bills. Early in March its Chairman, John Strutt, reported to the House that standing orders had been complied with. Thereupon Mr Roebuck and Mr Thomas Duncombe the MP for Finsbury were ordered to prepare the Bill and bring it in on 23 March. Ironically, Duncombe was known in the Commons as the 'champion of the unfortunate' through backing such causes as the defence of the Governor-General of Canada five years earlier and the imprisoned Chartists in 1840, as well as promoting the 'People's Petition' in 1842.

The Parliamentary Bill was duly presented but greeted with ridicule and utter scepticism by the House at the mere idea of man flying. However, the Speaker ordered a Second Reading, though with the same result, and the matter was dropped. Five days later the complete Patent was filed and published as No 9478 with full specification and schematic drawings. Nothing like it had ever been seen before. The double surfaced fabric covered huge monoplane wing spanning 150 ft had 26 great ribs carried on three main spars, for which the front and rear had scientifically located mid-span and central pylon trusses employing tension rods to take the wing bending strain. No identical contemporary form of this bracing was extant at that time although the principle was well-known, yet not only was it a pioneering form of bracing for a wing but also anticipated the 'cross-tree' rigging of Bermudan masted yachts of 70 years later. Equally noteworthy was the enclosed cabin featuring a pioneering tricycle undercarriage in the mode of the airliners of today.

The probability that the drawings were for a much smaller machine is emphasised by the detail of the tension wire assemlies, which are attached to a simple metal plate secured to the relatively thin spar wall with ten wood screws, and although there is a neat tensioning device foreshadowing the turnbuckle it is merely a threaded eyebolt and nut, and the wire shown on the detail drawing is of small piano wire diameter and not the oval section of a wider tie-rod defined in the specification 'to offer as little resistance as possible when passing through the air'.

Similarly the rectangular spars of the structural GA do not match the hollow ovals of the detail drawing intended to ensure 'lightness with sufficient strength' for the front and rear ones though the mid spar, described as 'main bar' was specified only as 'a plate of wood on edge' and was unbraced, yet the arrangement of compression ribs and drag bracing shows remarkable understanding and like the lift bracing became the standard technique of aircraft many decades later.

That the earlier experiments by Stringfellow and his young friend with gliding models had given them understanding of flight behaviour and control is indicated by the adjustable incidence of the big tail and a directional rudder, with a large central fin above the wing to give lateral stability, and the Henson patent confirms that model glider flights must have been made prior to 1842 by stating: 'From experiments, I have found it desirable that the weight should be forward' — and that is a major factor in securing longitudinal stability. Similar observation led to use of the adjustable tailplane so that 'the car may be caused to come to the earth in so flat an incline that very little shock (if any) will be perceived by the passengers'.

Modern calculations seem to confirm that the drawings might

originally have been intended as a light single-seater of not more than fifty feet span and ten feet chord which could just have had capacity for flight with the specified twenty-five to thirty nominal horse-power because its *brake* horse-power might be double that amount — though brake calibration was not yet a method of measurement. Instead, Henson was induced by Colombine as publicity promoter to give imagination rein and scale up the size, hopefully stating: 'From the various experiments I have been enabled to make there should be about one square foot for each half pound of weight of the machine, including machinery, fuel and load. The machine I am making will weigh about 3,000 pounds, and the surface of the planes of either side of the car will measure 4,500 square feet, and the tail 1,500 feet more.' On that scale the detail drawing shows the spar section of the centre bay as hollow ovals 6½ inches wide and 5 inches deep with walls 1¼ inches thick, and the solid central spar was approximately 10 inches by 2 inches; but stress investigation indicates that all assumptions of weight and structural safety factor were far too optimistic to be practicable, and the engine power utterly inadequate.

To what extent was the scientific John Chapman involved in all this? He had begun advising Henson on the steam engine Patent in 1840 for enrolment the following year, well aware that this power-plant was intended for a full-size flying machine based on winged models with which his client was experimenting, so in 1841 he must also have been working closely with him in preparing the Specification for the finalised *Ariel Steam Carriage* design which received its Provisional Patent on 29 September 1842. That he participated in formulating the design is endorsed by a letter he wrote eight years later to Sir John Guest, who was revising the British regulations for Patents: 'A very eccentric but observant and imaginative man of the name of Henson had made remarks on the action of the wind and on the flight of birds which led him to conceive the idea of a machine for flying founded on principles different from any which had previously been adopted. He was far too poor to pay for a patent, model etc., and fell into the hands of a party who had neither honesty nor discretion proportioned to the control which command of funds gave him.

'After some imperfect attempts with the models which had been constructed I was asked to investigate the matter. I soon found that the natural facts concerned with the resistance of the air were too little known from former investigations to serve for guidance. I instituted a large series of experiments with a machine different from any before employed by experimenters on this subject, from the results of which I inferred that Henson's invention, although not certain of success, had more probability of success than anything of the kind which had been done or proposed before.'

Chapman made no claim to dealing with the structural integrity of the machine, but some of his aviation papers discovered by his grandson in 1942, and others still in the family in the form of quarto notebooks, endorse that he was a considerable mathematician, though they deal primarily with propeller and aerofoil research. Unfortunately that 1942 collection disappeared after loan to J E Hodgson, a man of utmost integrity who was the Honorary Librarian of the Royal Aeronautical Society which in April 1943 published in their *Journal* an article by him on Henson based on these papers. In 1952 Hodgson died, so it seems possible that his Executors sold the Chapman papers believing they were his, as he operated a manuscript and antique book business, and it is certainly significant that in 1958 the Dickinson College, Pennsylvania, bought five boxes of Chapman's papers from Charles Hamilton, a manuscript dealer of New York, 'twenty five items on aeronautics having been removed from the corpus and sold separately'.

In October 1959 a collection of twenty-eight Chapman manuscripts of about 175 pages was auctioned in New York at the Parke-Bernet Galleries for $700 to Captain John Ide, who had been the representative in Paris of the USA's National Advisory Committee for Aeronautics. These documents were enclosed in a blue morocco folding case, inscribed on the backstrip 'Plans and letters for the Ariel Steam Air Carriage', and included the original draft specifications of the *Ariel* dated 16 August 1841 penned with many corrections on fifteen quarto pages in Chapman's hand except for the last two pages by Henson. Among other items were detailed descriptions of the machine, which was estimated to fly at fifty mph and have a range of 500 miles at full load; forty-five pages of reports to the financial backers; full accounts of aerodynamic aspects, propeller research, experiments in progress, nine folio sketches of various parts of the machine and appliances.

Two or three years later, Ide died and these Chapman papers again disappeared, but recently it has been ascertained that some went to the USA Library of Congress, others to un-named USA Universities, and some to the Smithsonian Institution. Subsequently it has been possible to obtain microfilms of those in the Library of Congress, and they prove to be those loaned to Hodgson, but do not include any relevant to the complex and skilled structural strength calculations which John Chapman, as a professional mathematician, must have done rather than Henson.

*   *   *

The almost simultaneous publication of the specification and the attempted Parliamentary Bill, coupled with an instantaneous propaganda campaign conducted by Colombine, caused every newspaper in the land and many a magazine, to make it the hilarious topic of the day. Comic songs, verses, caricatures, lampoons and critical articles appeared everywhere and the extravagant publicity gave cartoonists the opportunity of grotesquely imaginative illustrations picturing the 'Ariel Steam Carriage' flying the world's first air routes from London to Egypt and India — though Henson a decade later dismissed reports that his machine was designed to fly the Atlantic saying: 'This was mere newspaper talk. I never thought of anything so absurd.' Nevertheless, the subject aroused contentious discussion all over Europe. Philosophical and technical journals published articles in which men of science took sides for and against the idea of air transport.

The Times of 30 March 1843 commended the project in stately prose, declaring: 'Mr Henson says he has invented a machine by which men may traverse the untrammelled regions of the air in any direction at their pleasure. This is not the first time by many that such a pretention has been advanced: however failure, sometimes ridiculous, has always been the lot of the bold adventurers who had broodingly worked themselves into a determination to try out their schemes. Not one has succeeded, while all the world has at once longed for their success and derided their hopes. Nor do we now take the colour of our opinion of the sanguine character of the inventors as anticipation; yet we are compelled, by careful inquiry, to profess our belief that he has done so much towards simplifying the question on which the resolution of this momentous problem depends, and so much more towards removing the practical difficulties in the way of his accomplishment, that the earlier, if not immediate, possession of the long-coveted power of flight may now be safely anticipated.'

To criticisms of the design, Chapman replied with significant knowledge. On the pertinent question: 'What if the engine were to fail?' he explained that the aeroplane speed would be manipulated to give a landing shock no worse than jumping from a wall five or six feet high. To the suggestion that a storm might shatter the machine he pointed out that no gust could subject the wings, provided they were of adequate strength, to a pressure much greater than the weight of the machine, but the main effect of flying into a storm 'would be to retard its progress as measured from point to point', and in any case violent storms could be avoided by delaying the start. To the further objection that electricity in the clouds would be another threatening danger Chapman replied that 'the danger lies not in being highly charged with electricity but in being part of the circuit and before the Carriage reached the ground the charge would be greatly dissipated.'

The pundits particularly battled over the power necessary for flight after initial acceleration down the specially constructed 'inclined plane or a side of a hill' proposed by Henson to give sufficient speed for launching. Many critics wrote with argued logic, though their estimates of power for flight differed widely. Thus a commentator in the *Magazine of Science* for 1 April 1843 calculated that at least 100 hp would be required to propel the machine at 50 mph. Other estimates ranged up to 4,500 hp! Several pointed out that Henson had made insufficient allowance for the weight of fuel and water for any length of flight.

Shielded by his pseudonym 'LL', John Chapman also wrote in the *Mechanics Magazine* on April Fool's Day a glibly reasoned defence of Henson's Aerial Steam Carriage: 'We may confess at the outset that we were of the number of those who looked with incredulity on the announcement that Mr Henson had constructed a machine that would fly. . . In all probability if he had contented himself with demonstrating on paper that his machine, if constructed, would really travel through the air, he would have met with little attention; but he went so far, of himself, as to construct models of no inconsiderable magnitude, and these, we are told, exhibited capabilities so striking and unexpected that wealthy and influential persons were induced to encourage and support him.'

Chapman's entire comprehension of the structure and aerodynamics of Henson's machine is clear from the rest of his article in the *Mechanics Magazine,* for he gives extensive description of its construction and operation and a dissertation on the theory of inclined aerofoils and resultant forces, leading to his conclusion: 'We have only the probabilities for guidance; but as far as we can judge them they are in favour of Mr Henson's success.'

Cautiously playing it both ways, the editor added a sour note: 'We cannot see where the originality lies. The truth is that we can discover nothing of importance in the present scheme which has not been proposed and even tried before, with the exception perhaps of the steam boiler and even that seems to be rather a combination of known contrivances such as Vineys cones etc., than an embodiment of any original conceptions of Mr Henson's own.'

Coincidentally, Cayley had written to that magazine on 25 March, before the enrolment of Henson's specification, and recapitulated the principles of flight which he had published in 1810. The editor commented: 'No man living has bestowed more attention on the subject of aerostation than the philosophical Baronet has pursued through so long a course of years and with so much zeal and perseverance, nor is there anyone who has brought to the consideration of it more science or greater sagacity. Perhaps the greatest praise that could be bestowed on the present scheme of Mr Henson is that it happens to coincide so closely with the previous experiments and conclusions of so great an authority in such matters.' But it went far beyond that.

In the next issue of the *Mechanics Magazine*, Cayley wrote critically of Henson's machine: 'The extent of leverage, however well guarded by additional braces, is in this necessarily light structure, terrific. For though the wings are not intended to be wafted up and down, the atmosphere even in moderately calm weather near the earth, is subject to eddies; and the weight of the engine and cargo etc., in the central part of this vast extent of surface, would in the case of any sudden check, operate an enormous power to break the slender fabric.' He then questioned: 'Would it not be more likely to answer the purpose to compact the surface into the form of a three decker, each deck being 8 to 10 feet from each other, to give free room for the passage of air between them?'

On 22 April 'LL' replied with an article 'On the Objections to Mr Henson's Plan of Aerial Transit', commenting on and countering the Cayley criticism, re-iterating that 'Of all plans now before the public, Mr Henson's is, on the whole, likely to succeed,' and in the issue of 13 May he continued his attack against other objectors.

Chapman's 'Blue Notebook' reveals not only his extensive practical experimentation but also his commital to studying every treatise he could find on air resistance and the related subject of hydrodynamics. On 27 May the *Mechanics Magazine* published another article of his under the guise of 'LL' entitled 'Mechanical Flying — an Examination of the Theory of M Chabrier' which enabled him to make comparison between the powerful wing-beat used by a bird to take off and the small power needed by Henson's wings because of gravity assistance by running down an incline. Meanwhile *The Builder* magazine, which already had published a felicitous article about the *Aerial Carriage* (probably written by Chapman) sagely proposed in its issue of 6 May that the machine could more easily be launched from a railway truck with wings overhanging the track embankment.

Many other periodicals vaunted their views. Typically the *Civil Engineer and Architects Journal* devoted eighteen pages in May and June to criticising and dismissing the project, and on the basis of the air pressure tables of Rouse, Smeaton, and Hutton absurdly postulated that 'to secure permanent elevation would require 240 to 280 mph'. More rationally, the author affirmed that the structure 'would confound the best directed efforts of the most ingenious architect to combine solidity and lightness with the extension of a wing of any magnitude devoid of extrinsic source of support', and with foresight warned that: 'A dislocation or distention on one side more than the other of any of the numerous bracings by which rigidity of the plane is secured, must ensure an alteration in obliquity of flight with constant tendency to move in the circumference of a circle, which can only be resisted by a rudder of suitable dimensions.' And there, had Henson, Chapman, Stringfellow or Cayley perceived it, was the essence of wing-warping lateral control which eventually made aeroplanes practicable.

Chapter 4
Publicity Manoeuvring

Of Stringfellow's attitude during this time there is sparse record. His son Allan Harrison had been born on 19 May 1841, and that same year John was re-elected to Chard Council, whose Minute Book shows that he attended six meetings between June and October, eight in 1842 and six in 1843. A letter dated 18 November 1842 to the editor of the *Sherborne Journal* indicates how forthright he could be: 'Sir, Wolmer's *Exeter and Plymouth Gazette* of the 12 instant contains a statement to the effect that I voted against returning the amount of their non-attendance fines to the Alderman who resigned office here on the 9th instant. That it is a deliberate lie, and this is the fifth instance in which the lies told by the Chard correspondant of that paper, respecting persons there, have had to be publicly contradicted.'

Meanwhile Henson on his part was becoming discouraged both by the criticism of his project and lack of any financial support for the proposed Aerial Transit Company. On three occasions he had requested Colombine to abandon the project, and wrote to Stringfellow saying that he was 'sadly bothered in consequence of the parties with me not being mechanical men' and that he was 'wretchedly stinted for means'. Significantly he added 'I know the thing could easily be done if you and I were together.'

In hope of countering Sir George Cayley's criticism, Henson had a model of his Aerial Steam Carriage, styled as the *Ariel,* built for display at the Adelaide Gallery in the Strand, London, which was another Institution originally promoted by Sir George Cayley in 1830 for the edification of the public in various aspects of science by giving 20 minute lectures and demonstrations of models operated by steam or clockwork.

Writing on 26 June 1843 headed *Multum in Parvo,* and referring to a visit by Stringfellow, Henson wrote to the latter: 'I trust you arrived safe home though I have not heard from you to say so. The Adelaide model is not yet completed but everything connected with the framework was finished Friday last except the covering which will be finished tomorrow (Tuesday). Lodge made one engine but not very well, so he commenced another which will be finished Thursday or Friday and is the same in every respect but better made. The weight of the framework without the covering and the tail is 5 lbs and the weight of the engine without water and fuel is about 6 lbs. I expect the total weight to be about 13 lbs. I have made an improvement in the propellers of considerable importance. We expect to have an experiment about Friday. I think things are on a more settled and consequently satisfactory footing with Colombine. It will be at least another fortnight before I can come to Chard. I hope you are taking care of your health and not boring yourself to death and have adopted the cold bath. Recollect that health is worth taking care of. It is easy to keep well but difficult to get well. Hoping Mrs Stringfellow, Patty Anne, the little one and yourself are quite well. I am my dear Sir, Very Faithfully Yours.'

Reporting on the Adelaide experiments, the *Morning Herald* for 10 July 1843, declared that the first model had almost shaken itself to pieces in working, and continued: 'The second model engine is certainly a very novel thing. It consists of one cylinder only, and with its frame, water, fuel and firebox weighs but 6 lbs. This engine it is said performs 1,500 revolutions per minute. It does much credit to Mr Henson as well as the Institution at which it has been made.'

However, when it came to flight trials the *Herald* dismissively stated on 4 August: 'The experiments that have been made during the last two months at the Adelaide Gallery, with respect to this much be-puffed vehicle of communication between distant nations, would appear to be almost conclusive against the remotest probability of its ever performing an indoor trip beyond the rate of some 10 to 15 miles per hour.'

Henson's letters clarify that this was a steam engine model, and the paper confirmed that it had a horizontal surface (including tail area) of 40 sq ft and weighed 14 lbs. A lighter model of the same dimensions was therefore constructed and a much lighter and more powerful engine installed. An inclined plane, down which the model ran for launching, was made at one end of the gallery and parallel wires ran longitudinally at the other end to catch the model if it fell. In the first experiment as soon as the machine left the inclined plane it dropped onto these wires and the wing stays were broken. 'Not a single foot didn't fly,' the *Herald* disdainfully reported. A second attempt was made some days later with a still lighter engine, but was also a failure. 'A third, a fourth, and it is not likely known how many attempts were made, but with an invariable result. Directly the inclined plane was left the model came down flop. Up to the present time, therefore, the world is no nearer flying.'

However, a Henson letter to Stringfellow merely dated 'Wednesday evening' was more optimistic: 'I write in great haste

just to say that I did not get your last letter till the day before
yesterday when I visited home. I am now living in a tent on the
Hippodrome race course and was here all last week and the week
before.'

That course was at Bayswater, 2 miles from the end of Oxford
Street. He continued: 'I am extremely sorry that you should think
I had forgotten you as I shall always feel great pleasure in having
your friendship and I hope you will not think that I have wilfully
neglected you but attribute my silence to the real cause viz ex-
cessive worry, anxiety and want of time. I have not written a
letter to anyone for months, so pray don't let that interfere with
our friendship.

'I had (an attempt to) fly with my model on the 11th which was
highly satisfactory but not decisive. I don't at all fear but that I
shall succeed. It has caused an immense stir in London and I have
had congratulations from all quarters England, Ireland and Scotland. If you can come up to town I shall be glad to see you.
Accept my best thanks for the kind invitation you sent to me,
hoping you are well. Please remember me to Mrs Stringfellow and
Miss Patty.

'I have had a number of the nobility to see me who thought
themselves favoured by a special permission to see my apparatus.
When I go home again I will arrange to have my letters forwarded
to me. What have you done with your steam Engine?

'Believe me my dear Sir, your sincere friend.'

*　　*　　*

In the background, Chapman was conducting intensive research
throughout the summer of 1843. His several surviving notebooks
and loose sheets amount to over a hundred pages of data and
abstruse calculations using logarithms, differential calculus and
integration, and are an equivalent of the mathematics used for
structural stressing. There is analogous discussion of close-hauled
sailing and impulsions on sail and leeway, and references to
measurement of thrust produced by a suspended engine driving a
variety of propellers. Mention is made of tests with a spring-
powered model on 28 July; there is a note of a 12 ft 6 ins span
model of 4867 sq ins area, and of another weighing only '5 lbs 13
ozs with tail but without silk of about 2 ozs'. A delta-shape wing
is sketched and one 'which consists of a parallelogram close to
the body of half the length of the wing, and triangles of equal
length joined to the outer edge of the parallelogram' — but there
is no specific mention or drawing of the Aerial Carriage wing.

In an *ad interim* report of 10 October, John Chapman described

the open air experiments which he and Henson had made with a
'whirling arm carefully designed and accurately made' to determine 'atmospheric resistance on which the success or failure of
the Aerial Machine depend. . . . The friction of the machine itself
was ascertained by numerous and careful trials which were compared with the best recorded experiments, and the atmospheric
resistance due to the parts of the machine and the stems which
carried the Vanes (wings) were also carefully ascertained. . . The
number of experiments amounted to nearly 1,000, and a few of
them were recorded with less than five trials each.'

On 11th November Henson wrote to 44 year-old Stringfellow: 'I
dare say you think my long silence rather strange, but I waited to
have something decisive to tell you. We did not succeed at the
Adelaide Gallery for several reasons. The first engine was made
so badly that Lodge had to make another, and the framework
made by Swift was so anything but square that we threw it on one
side as useless. Since that time Mr Chapman and myself have
been making an extensive series of experiments (with an apparatus made on purpose) upon atmospheric resistance. These experiments quite bear out my theory and show that the old theory
was only right under certain circumstances. We also found that
the real power of the last engine made by Lodge (although better
than the first) was only half what it ought to be owing partly to the
natural difficulties attending more or less to all Models and the
want of delicacy on the part of the Adelaide man.

'I have been waiting for some time to come to Chard but I could
not think of allowing you to be at any expense without a chance of
remuneration, and while the experiments were going on it was not
in my power to bring them to any arrangement. All I could do was
to wait patiently for an opportunity, which I did not get till yesterday. I said I thought if a liberal offer was made to me I could find
someone who could carry out the Plan to success, and agreeably
to my proposition I am now enabled to offer you a repayment of
five times for all money or moniesworth in workmanship or
materials contributed by you to the amount of £200 — or, in other
words, if you like to enter into an agreement to undertake to make
a model with me in the way in which we talked about some time
since, I am at liberty to offer you five fold to be paid before anything else out of the first profits arising from Exhibition or other
way, for all money and work advanced and done. I have not time
to say more. Please send me an answer as early as possible. I just
add my firm conviction that you and I together can make the *Ariel*
fly. Hoping Mrs Stringfellow is in the best of health again. I am
dear Sir, very faithfully.'

Stringfellow's reply has not been discovered but can be surmised from Henson's next letter on 18 November: 'I think you are quite right in your views. I knew how you would feel on the matter, and I said distinctly whoever I might get to carry out the matter would expect to have control of it during progress and very liberal treatment also, and that in fact neither Colombine nor Marriott would know anything about it until it was done. If it succeeded they would have to fulfil the Contract, if not, they would hear no more about it. I shall leave a note at Colombine's today to ask him for a rough copy or sketch of the terms for you. Don't you think the buying of the Patent — I mean Colombine and Marriott's shares — would be a good move?'

Ten days later he wrote explaining that: 'Mr Colombine started for Ireland on Saturday and I did not get the wished-for letter, but I received a note from his cousin apologising for not sending it, giving as the reason that he was so pressed for time before he set off that he could not write to me till he returned but that I sufficiently understood his views and suggesting that I might be arranging matters with you and he would send me a letter when he returned. When I saw Mr C on Thursday last I told him the principle contents of your letters. I also proposed that you should have an interest in one or more of the following Patents and he was willing that you should have one (in addition to the five for one) or half of two such as those of France and Belgium. If you could come to town I have no doubt we could quickly come to some arrangement as Mr C is certain to be home again about the end of this week. If you cannot come, then all the writing will end in nothing I am afraid as it is impossible to understand each other by letter; besides it takes so much time.

'Our large engine is to be sold and the proceeds applied to experimenting and getting a Model to work. I would not ask you to spend any money about it if I did not feel sure it would be very advantageous to you as well as myself. The enclosed is a copy of the Terms on which we have already raised some money. If you don't come up, you must write and tell me your views or something decisive. Hoping yourself and Mrs Stringfellow are better.'

The engine referred to was a 20 nominal horse-power two cylinder of 7 ins bore and 14 ins stroke which together with boiler had been built for the full-size *Ariel* by Richard Houchin of City Road, London, who had been recommended to the consortium by John Farey CE, an eminent London engineer of those times who had written a treatise on steam engines and introduced a steam engine power indicator.

But now on 30 November the anxious Henson wrote again from 7 Ralph Place: 'I received your letter this morning and thought it better not to wait for C but to write you at once. Since I wrote on Tuesday I have learnt that he will be home on Saturday. There was something done towards attaining the foreign Patents some time since, but that is now void so it lies open to anyone and so far would be in favour of your plans. As it stands now, I have given away three-fifths of the capital, without getting it. In fact I cannot help feeling that I have been entrapped, a position which no honourable man would expect, for C knows as well as I that a certain sum of money was to have been advanced which has not been done, and he has said that he will not advance any more or take his money back and give it to some other person to carry out. The most I have been able to get from him is a mere verbal communication that he is willing to let other people do it on certain conditions. We shall see when he returns what he will do. He is willing to have an offer made to buy him out but he will not say what he will take, so here is truly realised the dog in the manger. Under these circumstances I certainly feel myself justified in using every means in my power to get out. What other course is there left?

'I can only say that I will do all in my power to see you amply repaid, and if C attempts to throw obstacles in the way then you and I will do the best we can without him, either with foreign patents or anything else which may be best. Therefore I will try and get you a note from C and if he does not attempt to take any further advantage, things may yet end all right; but if he does then I'll try what I can do, for I am resolved to get justice if possible.

'I am sorry your health will not permit you to come up to town, but if you will write and tell me what you propose I will settle it with C if I can, but if not without him. I forgot to say in my last that should you come to town you are welcome to half my bed if you can manage with that. Wishing you better health, I am my dear Sir, very faithfully yours. W S Henson. . . PS I cannot prevent the engine from being sold.'

On 8 December, Stringfellow's views evoked a despairing letter: 'I did not expect that you would agree to Mr C's proposal and I said in my second letter that I had no hopes of bringing you and C to an understanding — but then you hinted something might be done without him and I fell into your views in that respect because I felt justified in doing so. But you appear to have altered your mind about that part of the matter. In fact it is quite evident that your views are changed. There has been a month spent in fruitless correspondence and I cannot see we are any nearer the mark now than we were when we began. On the contrary we are further off than ever. The time makes no difference to you but it makes all the different to me. You have got a business to depend upon. I have not.

'Under these circumstances I do not feel justified, in fact I cannot carry on the correspondence any longer. I have done all I could towards forwarding the matter, therefore you must not blame me for taking this stand as the impression in my mind is that another month would still find us where we are now, and my present circumstances render it imperative that something be decided quickly. As I cannot do as I would, I must do as I can. I regret very much to be obliged to take this step as I think something might have been done if you had come to town, but I cannot help it and I hope it will not for a moment disturb the friendship which has hitherto existed between us. I shall at all times be happy to hear from you and shall be glad to see you when you come to town, or if at any time I can render you service I shall feel it a pleasure to do so. Hoping yourself and Mrs Stringfellow and family are well, I am, my dear Sir, very faithfully yours.'

Perhaps Stringfellow made conciliatory reply, for on 20 December Henson wrote, saying: 'My dear Sir, I just write today that I will do the pleasure of seeing you tomorrow afternoon. I shall start from Paddington at quarter past ten in the morning for Taunton. I don't know yet how I shall get to Chard from Taunton. I am dear Sir, Yours etc.'

Discussions must have gone well. Following the Christmas Festival they signed a mutually joint Agreement on 29 December stating that:-

'Whereas it is intended to construct a model of an Aerial Machine to be employed in such manners the parties above-named shall consider best and most profitable.

1st. It is agreed if considered necessary, to take out Patents for the same jointly, but be it understood that this Agreement does not extend to England except to such parts that are improvements upon Patents already taken out in England.

2nd. That all monies advanced to be considered as lent to be deducted from the profits that may arise hereafter.

3rd. That all profits after deducting expenses be equally divided.

4th. That it is the intention of the agreement that the parties above-named shall be on perfect equality as regards carrying out and working the same.

5th. That it is intended at a future time, if considered necessary and desirable, to enter into an Agreement more definite and explicit, according as circumstances may arise to require it.

6th. That the parties hereby pledge themselves in honour to each other to do all that lies in their power towards carrying out the object of this Agreement.

7th. That nothing herein mentioned shall be construed into a partnership beyond carrying out jointly the object of this Agreement.'

Chapter 5
Trial and Tribulation

Early in 1844 the thirty-two year-old bachelor Henson moved back to Chard, but as his address is not in the local Trade Register of that year it is possible he lodged with John Stringfellow to afford closest co-operation. There is no contemporary record of how they tackled their project, only the imprecise account written by Stringfellow's son Frederick John almost fifty years later — but at the time of the ensuing flight attempts he was only a twelve year-old school boy. His recollection was that: 'They commenced the construction of a small model operated on by a spring.' Possibly it had the small wings standing against the studio wall in the background of two of the photographs in the Stringfellow collection, or the model may have been an ornithopter because he states: 'An engine was also made for this model, and a wing action tried but with poor results.'

What is certain is that his father and Henson subsequently 'laid down a larger model twenty feet from tip to tip of the planes, 3½ feet wide, giving seventy square feet of sustaining surface, and about 10 more in the tail', and it was based on scaled-down drawings of those in Henson's patent specification. From uncertain memory of boyhood Fred Stringfellow stated: 'The planes were stayed from the three sets of fish-shaped masts, and rigged square and firm by flat steel rigging. The engine and boiler were put in the car to drive two screw propellers, right and left handed, three feet in diameter, with four blades each occupying three-quarters of the area of the circumference, set at an angle of sixty degrees'.

The machine and its pioneering propellers were an astounding forecast of the future aeroplane because it had all the essential elements except that of lateral control — yet even there the central top fin shows that the difficulty of lateral instability was as well known to Henson and Stringfellow as those of directional and longitudinal requirements catered for by tailplane and rudder, for the fin high above the CG would give a righting effect when the machine rolled and sideslipped; in fact, full-scale, the machine could have been flown as a two-control aeroplane.

There is no indication that months and months went by other than the comment: 'The making of this model required great consideration; various supports to the wings were tried, so as to combine lightness with firmness, strength and rigidity. A considerable time was spent in perfecting the motor power. Compressed air was tried and abandoned. Tappets, cams and eccentrics were all tried to work the slide valve to obtain the best results.'

Though this must have been spread over a long period, the framework of the twenty-foot span *Ariel* structure could easily have been completed within a few months, but probably both men were undertaking the project as spare-time work. Certainly Stringfellow had his engineering business to attend to, let alone his other hobbies and considerable research on the subject of electricity. But how Henson was employed has defeated investigation, though others were aware of his work as indicated by letters from the wife of the Mayor of Exeter who wrote to him on 29 March 1844: 'The interest I have from the first taken in your important discovery will I hope excuse my taking the liberty of addressing you. I was lately informed that you were in our neighbourhood — for such I consider Chard to be — and I am desired by my husband to say that if you can come to this city I shall be very happy to make your acquaintance instead of waiting for a more formal introduction from our friend Mr Fred Marriott. We both feel anxious to hear some news of the progress in perfecting the Aerial Steam Carriage having understood that you are still steadily working at it. The general opinion is that the thing has certainly failed but it is not over, and as we know you never were so sanguine as Mr M we believe that from you we should learn what the real prospects are at present.

'Wishing the favour of your reply, and with our united wishes for your ultimate success. Yours truly & obliged, Anne Drewe.'

On 5 April the lady wrote again: 'I received your letter and am very sorry I delayed writing until you had left our immediate neighbourhood. I hope however you can still make it convenient to run down, if only for a day or two, as both Mr Drewe and myself are very anxious to hear from the fountain head full particulars relative to your great and most interesting Invention. If however your engagements should prevent you, will you oblige me by letting me know what is the impediment now as to the success of the Steam Carriage and whether you are going on with your experiments in your present residence at Chard. I deeply regret you should have been deserted by those you say ought to have supported it now at the eleventh hour, but hope your patience and perseverance meet with full appreciation and reward. With our united compliments and hoping to hear from you in a day or two, I remain Sir, Yours truly.'

No reply has been found, and by the end of the year it is clear that Henson had returned to London, leaving Stringfellow to finish the work.

Thus on 24 April 1845 Stringfellow wrote to him with the usual 'My dear Sir': 'It is now some time since I heard from you. How are you getting on? I very much regret this fine weather passing as it could not be better for outdoor experiments. I did not get the thin Iron for making the engine fireplace till about a fortnight since. However I have completed it and tried the 28 cone boiler and don't find it sufficient to keep up the steam as it ought to with the tappets as it was when you left. I have since put on an excentric and fixed the engine all right in the Machine, also made some alterations in the valve. I tried it yesterday and consider it far superior to anything we have done before, so there is now no vibration. Whether this is to be attributed all to the excentric or partly to the alteration made in the valve, I can't say.

'I had 64 ounces of water in, and 14 ounces of Spirits and have no doubt it would have carried the machine off the ground from level rail as it had a strong inclination to carry it out of the window! I worked the engine from 15 to 20 minutes — burnt out the spirits and had about 14 ounces of water left. Give me your opinion of the next step to be taken.

'Since writing the above I have been busy. I don't know if I must infer from your letter that you are now at liberty for a short period, so it would be very desirable to make some outdoor experiments this spring, but it would be desirable to make another pair of propellers first.

'I have also made a nice little air-walking stick of iron, about 1lb in weight and little more than three-quarters of an inch in diameter to shoot small balls. It shoots harder than the large stick. I also made a pretty little Sunday purse to carry in your watch pocket if it is deep enough.

'There is a large party on Pilsdon Hill. They are erecting a tower or something of the sort. I have not yet been up, but shall go the first opportunity. Perhaps they may build a house big enough to hold the machine, which would be very handy. I believe they are building one of some sort. Yours very Truly. PS. We have had an increase in our family about 6 weeks since.' That was the birth of Edward Theodore on 16 March.

Pilsdon, some ten miles from Chard, is the tallest hill in Dorset, over 900 feet high, and crowned with a multi-ditched neolithic camp giving far distant views across the countryside. His reference to 'the machine' must have referred to the twenty-foot *Ariel,* for which a location at Pilsdon would have been very suitable for experimental flights, but the reference seems to infer that the big model still was not ready.

Stringfellow's next letter of 16 May is puzzling, and though unaddressed it is apparently to Henson and may indicate that the latter was helping his remarkable friend John Chapman with the latter's proposals for construction of a great Indian Peninsular Railway for which a company of that name had been opened at 3 New Broad Street.

After describing further experiments with the engine Stringfellow asks: 'How are you going on with your Railway Bill? I hope you still succeed. Shall be glad to see you at Chard as soon as you can make it convenient. When do you think I may expect you? We buried poor Phillip Yacey on Wednesday. He was seized with a fit of apoplexy down at Riste's lace factory at 12 o'clock on 8th inst., and died about 4 o'clock the same day. You never name your father. I hope he is getting on well. Hoping to hear from you soon.'

William Henson senior and family had recently migrated from Clerkenwell to America and settled in Newark, New Jersey where he 'contrived considerable improvements in carpet machinery'.

Possibly to gain more free time for the *Ariel* model, Stringfellow resigned from Chard Council after its meeting on 20 May. That intense engine development was taking place is indicated by surviving records of tests of a single cylinder unit with piston rods passing through the ends of the cylinder and the long connecting rods worked direct on the crank of his propellers. The diameter of the cylinder was 1½ inches and the piston had a three inch stroke. Typically Stringfellow recorded:–

> June 27 1845. Water 50 oz., spirit 10 oz., lamp lit 8.45, gauge moves 8.46, engine started 8.48 (100 lb pressure) engine stopped 8.57, worked 9 minutes, 2,288 revolutions average 254 per minute. No priming, 40 oz. water consumed, propulsion (thrust of propellers) 5 lb. 4½ oz. at commencement, steady at 4 lb. ½ oz., 57 revolutions to 1 oz. water, steam cut off one third from beginning.

*   *   *

On 25 July Stringfellow wrote to Henson telling him: 'I am not waiting for the silk as I have done nothing to the second pair of propellers for the large machine and am sorry to say I have been otherwise employed for the last week — that is, in repairing a Disaster! Last Monday week in the morning I found the trap fallen on the floor, one of the cords having broken in two at a point where there appeared to be a little iron mould. Like all other bad jobs it might have been worse. I don't find any damage done to the framework of the Machine, only the Boiler broken from its bearing and the dome and steam gauge budged a good deal. I had the frame and propellers of the small machine underneath it at the time which was literally smashed to pieces and I have now been spending my time for more than a week on it. I have succeeded in making it fully strong if not quite so light and neat. Meanwhile I am glad to hear you have been fully employed and got your Bill through the Committee of the Lords.

'I have also received two notes from Marriott; in the one received this morning there was a proposition which I give you under and to which I believe Colombine is agreeable. That is to divide the Patent interests into 12 as follows, Henson 4/12, Colombine 4/12, Marriott 2/12, Stringfellow 2/12. This Marriott thinks equable and just. I refrain from giving you my opinion on the subject as I should wish your opinion on it candidly and unbiased. He also purposed a meeting same as you mentioned in your letter and wishes my answer by return of post, but of course I shall give him no answer until I hear from you.'

Nevertheless all this was visionary. The company had no assets, though the ratios of sharing indicate the relative importance of each partner's participation. Thus Colombine as promoter is on level footing with Henson the inventor, and Marriott the publicity man is equated with Stringfellow the constructor and engine expert.

According to Stringfellow's eventual friend and confidant Frederick W Brearey, writing almost a quarter of a century after the event, the machine was at last ready for trials in 1845, so the year 1847 given decades later by Stringfellow's son Fred may relate only to a particular trial, or the date may be a misapprehension after the many years preceding publication.

However, the actual year is not important, but it is lamentable there are no contemporary descriptions of the crucial testing of the impressive twenty-foot span monoplane, for it was as big as some of the man-carrying midget racing aeroplanes of today, nor is there evidence that Henson participated in these trials despite their obvious importance in relation to his still hoped-for project of building a full-sized passenger carrier.

Stringfellow was anxious to avoid crowds and onlookers, so the dismantled machine was loaded on a haywain and his workmen took it secretly by night up Snowdon Hill highway westward of his house, and at the fork by the turnpike proceeded through secluded lanes to a big tent they had erected on unfrequented Bewley (also known as Bala) Down two miles from Chard.

He was well aware from observation of birds and the small hand-launched models with which he had emulated them in the late 1830s that heading into a breeze was essential for quick take-off, so a moveable sloping ramp was constructed, down which the model would slide to attain sufficient flight speed in the manner described by Henson in his patent. Certainly there must have been helpers to assemble and manhandle the model, for it comprised a bulky seventy square feet of surface, though only weighed thirty pounds. Probably his fourteen year-old son Frederick John was there on several occasions for he recollected long afterwards, 'The experiments were not as favourable as expected. The machine could not support itself for any distance, but when launched off, gradually descended.' Major problems must have arisen because with no pilot to move the elevator tailplane at appropriate time when going down the ramp, the machine would go straight on into the ground, or if the tail had been set at sufficient negative incidence for a change of attitude to take-off incidence, it would probably continue briefly rising until momentum was lost, then stall and drop wing-first into the ground with a degree of damage which might take days to repair. Brearey stated that seven weeks elapsed with attempt after attempt, including attention to engine and propellers, without sign that the machine could support its own weight, so the trials were abandoned.

Two decades after these attempts Fred Brearey, as part of his duties as Secretary of the Aeronautical Society of Great Britain, visited Stringfellow, and writing in an 1869 issue of *Popular Science Review* said that the seventy year-old pioneer told him: 'There stood our aerial protégée in all her purity — too delicate, too fragile, too beautiful for this rough world; at least those were my ideas of the time, but little did I think how soon it was to be realised. I soon found, before I had time to introduce the spark, a drooping of the wings a flagging in all the parts. In less than 10 minutes the machine was saturated with wet from a deposit of dew, so that anything like a trial was not possible by night. I did not consider we could get the silk tight and rigid enough. Indeed the framework was all too weak. The steam engine was the best part. Our want of success was not for want of power or sustaining surface, but for want of proper adaptation of the means to the end of the various parts.'

That was probably an abbreviation of what the old man said in describing the first attempt at flight, but apart from reference to the engine, takes no cognisance of the next seven weeks of experimentation which undoubtedly must have taken place by day with tight fabric, though the necessity for calm conditions would have swiftly become apparent because laterally and directionally the machine had little stability except that induced by the central top fin and fixed rudder. In fact Brearey must have been told by Stringfellow himself that: 'Many trials by day down inclined guide rails showed a faulty construction, and the model's lightness proved an obstacle to its successful contending with the ground current' — which at least indicates that at times it became airborne, though descending.

Brearey adds the comment that: 'Pictorial illustrations of the machine were widely published at the time.' None have been traced, so he may have been referring to those of the 1843 spate of picturesque drawings based on the *Ariel* patent specification. Unfortunately photography was merely in the early stages of experimental development, and the idea of a camera which could produce negatives for reproduction printing had only recently been conceived, though the Daguerreotype was in vogue for portraiture using a sensitised silver plate and long exposure, resulting in a single positive that could not be reproduced.

Chapter 6

Epochal Independent Success

By now Henson was at his wits' end over finance, and in a last attempt to secure money had written on 28 September 1846 to seventy-three year-old Sir George Cayley: 'Although I am personally unknown to you I have taken the liberty of addressing you this letter upon Aerial Navigation knowing it to be a subject in which you, as well as myself, feel deeply interested. You probably imagined that I had long since given it up as a failure, but you will be pleased to hear that I have in conjunction with my friend Mr Stringfellow been working more or less since 1843 towards the accomplishment of Aerial Navigation, and that we feel very sanguine as to the result of our endeavour and consider we have arrived at the stage which justifies us in obtaining that pecuniary assistance necessary to carry on our efforts upon an enlarged scale and with increasing energy. We therefore resolved to apply to you as the Father of Aerial Navigation to ascertain whether you would like to have anything to do with the matter or not. We have conducted our experiments in a strictly private manner and trust you will consider this communication to be the same. We find steam power ample for our purpose but of course we should not confine ourselves to it if your Air Engine offers superior advantages.'

The admission of corporate endeavour with Stringfellow is important evidence in view of assessments by the Science Museum's pre-war director and subsequent writers giving Henson all the credit.

A fortnight later Cayley replied: 'I had thought that you had abandoned the subject, which though true in principle you had rushed upon with far too great confidence as to its practise some years ago. If you have been making experiments since that time you will have found how many difficulties you have to adjust and overcome before the results you wish can be accomplished. I think that Balloon Aerial Navigation can be done readily and will probably come into use before Mechanical Flight can be rendered sufficiently safe and efficient for ordinary use.

'I like your zeal, and as you seem disposed to treat me with your confidence I can assure you that I shall not abuse it. As to new principles, there are none. Of practical expedience there will soon be an endless varity, and to select the best is the point at issue. I hope to be in No. 20 Hertford Street the latter end of November or beginning of December, when if you can show me any experimental proof of mechanical flight maintainable for a sufficient time by mechanical power, I shall be much gratified. Though I have not the weight of capital to apply to such matters, I perhaps might be able to aid you in some measure by my experience, or connection with other mechanical persons. I do not however think that any money, except by exhibition of a novelty can be made by it.'

Nevertheless the correspondence seems to have triggered Cayley into renewed interest in the possibilities of Aerial Navigation, for his notebook entry of 30 August three years later records: 'I tried some experiments with a view to ascertain with accuracy the real angle that any plane makes with its line of flight when supporting a given weight, and also the power shown to be necessary in that line of flight to sustain that weight. The surface was 16 sq ft of cotton cloth tightly stretched by two spars like those of a ship's sail laid horizontally to give little resistance to the air.'

Meanwhile Stringfellow's efforts at raising capital were as unsuccessful as Henson's when he tried to interest John B Gifford, the largest employer of labour for lace manufacture in Chard, for he was told: 'Now Mr Stringfellow, give up this nonsense. God never meant man to fly and we never shall fly.'

That was the end of the *Ariel* as far as Henson was concerned. Early in 1847 he was known to be in London, and was living at 27 New City Chambers, Bishopsgate, in the latter part of the current year. The next news of William Samuel was that he had patented a safety razor.

Despite his many preoccupations, Stringfellow gave another lecture on electricity on 17 June 1847, again revealing his fluent command of English and extensive research, typically referring to seven works on that subject written between 1600 and 1779: 'Electricity,' he said, 'is no longer the paltry confined Science which it was once fancied to be, making its appearance only from the function of glass or wax employed in childish purposes, serving as a trick for the schoolboy, or a nostrum for the quack. It has proved to be intimately connected with all operations in chemistry, with magnetism, with light and colour. It is apparently a property belonging to all matter, ranging through all space from sun to sun, planet to planet.'

The subject of electricity was interesting many people of scientific outlook, and among those with whom Stringfellow made contact was the celebrated Andrew Crosse, Squire of Fyne

Court, at Broomfield on the Quantocks, where he was locally known as the 'thunder and lightning man' because on occasion his experiments produced brilliant flashes and deafening bangs, scaring the villagers out of their wits. They believed he had sold his soul to Satan. His researches attracted many prominent scientists of the time, including Sir Humphrey Davey, Sydney Smith, and Von Liebig. From time to time Crosse visited String-fellow at his house because of their mutual interest and there were reciprocal journeys to Fyne Court.

Stringfellow was also continuing his own independent aero-nautical investigations, for in 1846 he had already begun making a small engine and multi-tube boiler to drive the twin propellers of an envisaged smaller monoplane with swallow-shaped wings which he had correctly deduced were more efficient in giving a flatter glide due to lower drag than the rectangular form which Henson adopted, and therefore less power would be required for sustained flight.

There is doubt as to the size of this flying model, which was finished early in 1848 — for it took considerable time and meticu-lous work to make a small engine and obtain efficient thrust from the propellers and drive. Stringfellow's son Fred was not yet six-teen and it was not until he was sixty that he retrospectively drew on what must have been imprecise recollection of those early years as a teenager and stated that: 'The aero-planes were about 10 ft from tip to tip and 2 ft at the widest part tapering to a point, slightly curved on the under- surface, rigid in front, feathered at the back,' and by that he meant flexible trailing edge.

Photographs taken very much later when glass-plate negatives were standard, throw doubt as to the span of the model. If the wing spread is scaled up from the width of the chair on which the model rests, say 18 inches, the span is of the order of twelve feet. But in 1892 Frederick John confusingly also stated: 'My father had constructed another small model, which was finished early in 1848, and having the loan of a long room of a disused lace factory, the small model was moved there early in June for experiments. The aero-planes of this model were about 10 ft from tip to tip.'

Confusion is also compounded because in that same booklet he gives the weight as 'under 9 lbs', yet Brearey, writing twenty-three years earlier in *Popular Science Review*, based on dis-cussion with old John himself, gives 6 lbs, and with water and fuel did not exceed 6½ lbs. Frederick John gives the area as 14 sq ft, but Brearey states 17 sq ft, and a reconstruction of the model in-dicates 18 sq ft. However the size is not of fundamental import-ance nor are the dimensions of the steam-engine which had a ¾ ins diameter cylinder and stroke of 2 ins, but its degree of power was vital and so was the propeller efficiency.

The machine had no vertical tail surface, so would have been directionally unstable in gusts, and the relatively deep nacelle of similar shape to that of the *Ariel* cabin could induce both directional and lateral instability, but John Stringfellow was well aware of these factors because of his open air trials with the *Ariel* model, so he confined his experiments to the still air of a room about 22 yards long. For effective launching, he abandoned the idea of a steeply descending ramp and ingeniously suspended the model from a tandem-wheeled frame running on a downward inclined wire along which it traversed several yards before encountering a block which released the winged machine for a short free flight.

In his 1892 account Frederick John enlarged on Brearey's 1869 description of the tests: 'The inclined wire for starting the machine occupied less than half the room and left space at the end for the machine to clear the floor. In the first experiment the tail was set at too high an angle, and the machine rose too rapidly on leaving the wire. After going a few yards it slid back, as if coming down an inclined plane at such an angle that the point of the tail struck the ground and was broken. The tail was repaired and set at a less angle. The steam was again got up, the machine started down the wire and upon reaching the point of self-detachment, gradually rose until it reached the farther end of the room, striking a hole in the canvas placed to stop it.'

That was the first power-driven self-supported flight in world history. Stringfellow must have been quietly jubilant, for he had achieved success where his younger friend Henson had failed. Henson in fact had faded from the picture. He had been courting a 25 year-old young lady, Sarah Anne Jones, and married her at the Church of Saint Botolph Aldgate on 4 March 1848. Meanwhile his father was active in the USA and successfully urged William Samuel to emigrate there in view of expanding opportunities in the New World, so on the morning of 31 March the couple boarded the square rigger *Mediator* at London Dock and set sail for New York where they arrived at 10 am on 5 May. Next day they crossed the Hudson River to Newark where they were met by his father and mother, sisters and brothers. In October William Samuel 'went to Mr Kentons to work at steam engines and drawings etc'. For the rest of his days his home was at Newark, though he ventured on business as far as Mexico and Peru.

Meanwhile Stringfellow had been conducting further flights with his model, some of which were witnessed by his sons, and Frederick John recorded in much later Victorian times: 'In experiments the machine flew well, rising as much as 1 in 7. The late J Riste Esq., lace manufacturer, Northcote Spicer Esq., J Toms Esq. and others witnessed the experiment. Mr Marriott (late of the *San Francisco Newsletter*) brought from London Mr Ellis the then lessee of Cremorne Gardens, Mr Partridge, and Lieutenant Gale RN the aeronaut to witness experiments. Mr Ellis offered to construct a covered way at Cremorne for further experiments. Mr Stringfellow repaired to Cremorne, but not much better accommodation that he had at home was provided owing to unfulfilled engagements as to room.'

The reference to the *Newsletter* is out of context in the chronological sequence because it was not published until written in relation to 1892. Of the quoted witnesses at Chard, John Riste was senior partner in the lace business of Wheatley and Riste, had been a Borough Councillor with Stringfellow since 1842, and was twice Mayor of Chard; Northcote W Spicer of Snowdon Cottage Lane was a doctor similarly prominent on the Borough Council and had been Mayor in 1842 at the time of the Chartist Riots; John Toms lived in a large house at the corner of Holywood Street and Fore Street and had been Mayor in 1838, his business activities embracing postmaster, printer, stationer, insurance agent, grocer and ironmonger. However, though doubtless impressed by what they saw, these worthies unfortunately left no written evidence.

Mr Ellis proved as good as his word. With commendable speed a sizeable open tent-like structure was erected on a grassy space in the Cremorne Gardens where Lord Cremorne formerly lived in a mansion in his Thames-side estate of fourteen acres abutting Kings Road, Chelsea. Recently it had all been sold to a consortium and was now operated by Mr Ellis as pleasure grounds open to a fee-paying public, and provided open air entertainment on summer evenings with spectacular events such as balloon ascents, the first of which had been by a Mr Hampton in 1839.

Ellis announced to the local Press: 'CREMORNE Aerial Steam Navigation — the Lessee has the honour to announce he has concluded arrangements for an exhibition of models, worked by steam power, without the aid of gas, and illustrative of the preliminary step of this new movement of the age.'

That was followed by an advertisement in *The Illustrated London News* of 19 August 1848: 'CREMORNE. Aerial Steam Navigation and Balloon Night ascent. On Monday August 21 Lieutenant Gale will make another night ascent at 10 o'clock, and discharge from the car a magnificent display of fireworks. Flights of the Aerial Carriage between three and six o'clock. Previous to each a brief explanatory lecture will be delivered.'

The Times of 22 August reported: 'A series of experiments were made beneath an immense hood or awning in Cremorne Gardens yesterday afternoon to test the powers of a machine invented by Mr Stringfellow to maintain and propel itself through the air. The day was most unpropitious and it would be hardly fair to pass judgment on the powers of the machine to carry out the assertions of the inventor compared with those who have witnessed it under more favourable circumstances. It certainly possesses a propelling power and it would appear that with the addition of a sustaining power it might form an important aid to aerial or balloon experiments. A great many scientific gentlemen and others connected with inventions were present. The attempts will be repeated tomorrow and as the thing is rather more than ordinary interest, the Friends of Science have an opportunity of forming their own judgement of its worth.'

Forty years later Frederick John's recollection was more favourable: 'Mr Stringfellow was preparing for a departure when a party of gentlemen unconnected with the Gardens begged to see an experiment, and finding them able to appreciate his endeavours, he got up steam and started the model down the wire. When it arrived at the spot where it should leave the wire it appeared to meet with some obstruction, and threatened to come to the ground, but it soon recovered itself and darted off in as fair a flight as was possible to make a distance of about 40 yards, where it was stopped by the canvas.' That extended distance certainly proved the machine's potential for sustained flight.

Explaining why this situation was not · further developed, Frederick John in that recollective Victorian report of his says, 'Having now demonstrated the practicability of making a steam engine fly, and finding nothing but a pecuniary loss and little honour, this experimenter rested for a long time, satisfied with what he had effected. The subject, however, had for him special charms, and he still contemplated renewal of his experiments.'

That paragraph was in fact merely an imaginative effort to cover a lapse of time in which Frederick John was absent from the scene for the next fifteen years except for two brief visits.

Chapter 7
Continuing Development

Mail arriving at the Stringfellow home late in 1848 from Galveston, Texas, broke the news that Mrs John Stringfellow's father, Thomas Keetch, had died, and that his widow, Ellen Keetch needed help in sorting out the estate and running his business of chemist and medical supplier. He had originally come from Newfoundland where his daughter Hannah had been born but she was eventually sent to England for her education under the care of an aunt at Wadeford, 1½ miles from Chard, where she lived until her marriage. Hannah grieved at the loss of her father and predicament of her mother, but as a mother herself with a large family she could do nothing to help, so to allay her concern her husband agreed to take their young son Frederick John to Galveston to assist with the shop.

Early in 1849 father and son set sail on the long, slow, sea journey of more than 5,000 miles to the fine harbour of Galveston Island in the Gulf of Mexico some 300 miles south-west of New Orleans. This was a growing and important port, exporting cotton, oil, corn and timber of a high annual value. Typical of the township were the wooden houses built on stilts as a safeguard against the flooding caused by occasional hurricanes.

It is very unlikely that the Stringfellows were accompanied by Frederick Marriott, that disastrous entrepreneur of the abortive Aerial Transit Company, but he also arrived in the USA at about this time, heading for the West Coast where he was subsequently closely associated with affairs in San Francisco. Certainly he had no intention of visiting the now hostile William Samuel Henson en route or there would have been mention of this in the latter's diary which on 18 April of that year records the birth of Stella Henson, his first daughter.

How long John Stringfellow stayed in Texas is not known, but these were the days of the 'Gold Rush' in California — a far journey across the largely unexplored Western outback of mountain and desert that was not yet one of the States of the Union. The stories of the miners, those 'forty-niners', greatly interested him, for the talk everywhere was of rich deposits easily worked. Here was a chance to achieve the capital which he and Henson had so fruitlessly sought for the construction of their man-carrying aeroplane. Wisely he decided first to return to England to check that his Chard business was operating satisfactorily before venturing on the great gold rush trek to California. Young Frederick John meanwhile could stay with his grandmother Keetch.

Rather than make the arduous voyage home by sailing ship, John Stringfellow may well have taken the recently opened railroad from New Orleans to New York, thence to England by the recently introduced paddle-steamers operated by Samuel Cunard, a Nova Scotian sailing ship owner who had boldly entered the Atlantic trade in 1840, but whose ships were now of more than 1,000 tons and could average a steady 8½ knots. Certainly the great steam engines and their ponderously moving crank shafts and piston rods would have been of enthralling interest to John Stringfellow, but despite what seemed their enormous power, the journey would still take fourteen days to three weeks depending on whether there was a following or a head wind.

Probably it was late summer when he arrived back in Chard. All was well until Hannah learned of the possibility of his absence to seek gold in a foreign land for a year or more, and presently she fell ill, or feigned it. That was too much for John, and he abandoned the prospect, but his oldest son William Henry, a lazy youth of 20, who had always been a problem, grasped at the chance of untrammelled freedom with reward of riches and induced his parents to let him go instead. Late in 1849 he left for the USA only to vanish and was never heard of again.

That left young Fred at Galveston with his grandmother, but he was happy there. In the ensuing months not only was he the greatest help in running the shop but also learned the rudiments of becoming a chemist, possible helped by H C L Aschoff who owned a wholesale and retail chemical business in Market Street, Galveston.

Meantime the Hensons had become firmly established at Newark, New Jersey, and in due course became full citizens of the USA. As recorded by S Paul Johnston, the directories of that city carried a continuous record of his residence there and he was variously described as engraver, mechanical draughtsman, artist and civil engineer. During the 1850s he worked for a time with the Newark Machine Co and for one year listed himself as the 'William S Henson & Co., Machinists and Engineers, Union Building, Corner of Mulberry and River'. In the following year he appears simply as 'Draughtsman, Newark Machine Company'. There was no record of any continuing interest in aviation other than obtaining a pamphlet by Solomon Andrews, dated 22 July 1848, which proposed an 'Association of Inventors of Aerial Devices'.

His erstwhile mentor John Stringfellow at 50 still found time to begin a new flying model, despite the demand for improved bobbin-lace machines and was exporting occasional small industrial steam engines to the Continent although the third French Revolution had broken out in Paris in 1848, causing King Louis Philippe to flee to England. The throne of nearly every monarch in Europe began to totter, but Queen Victoria had become the established idol of the British public. However in Ireland there was agitation, verging on rebellion for the repeal of the Union with England.

Undisturbed, Chard was pursuing its own quiet way. Half the 5,000 population were gainfully employed, though a large percentage were children working at the lace mills, of which Holyrood Mill was the biggest with a six storey high brick factory; however the Lower Mill operated by Wheatley, Riste & Wheatley, whose original mill had pioneered the lace industry in Chard, was nearly as big and Stringfellow still maintained close contact there. As a worker in iron he would have been closely acquainted with John Whiteman and John Smith who had separately set up local iron foundries; and of smaller industries there were the carpenters and masons of the building trade, cabinet makers, coach builders and wheelwrights, coopers for the increasing cottage industry of brewing and a host of lesser activities such as brush making, basket weaving, sack making, rope making, printing and clock-making. Encircling Chard was increasingly productive agricultural activity, but the wage of a farm labourer did not exceed 8s a week for a 6 am to 6 pm stint, and boys might earn 1s 6d.

Roads during the past two decades had greatly improved, and a road mender hammering away at large stones for re-surfacing was a commonplace sight on every journey, but the highways were still subject to payment at the turnpike. For every horse drawing a wheeled passenger-carrying vehicle the charge was 6d; those drawing wagon, wain or cart paid 3d; any unladen beast was 1½d, and a drove of oxen or cows cost 10d per score.

Of local amenities there was the new facility of piped water instead of depending on wells or the stream gushing down the main street and the pavements were now illuminated at night. The Mail Coach left the George Inn every week-day morning for Taunton, via Ilminster; another for Bristol, Exeter and the north; and the London mail left at 7 pm each evening. There was also a remarkable extensive network of private carrier cart services to London and other distant parts, daily to Taunton and three times a week to Exeter, Yeovil, Axminster and coastal places such as Lyme Regis. Bulk goods were carried by the Chard canal via various inclines and tunnels to the Taunton and Bridgwater canal which had opened in 1842, but Chard was still without a direct railway, though the Bristol and Exeter line, which had also opened in 1842, now provided eight passenger and two luggage trains a day calling at Taunton, so the Borough Council was considering an approach to the directors of the South Western in hope of attracting a direct line from Yeovil to Exeter stopping at Chard.

In this world of accelerating progress John Stringfellow had many friends in all grades of society except the nobility. Like all Victorians he now had a large family, but of the twelve children only nine reached maturity. From Frederick John across the sea in Galveston there must have been letters from time to time, but no correspondence has survived, though an archivist at the Galveston Library in 1950 by chance discovered a bill of exactly 100 years earlier 'Payable to the Estate of Thomas Keetch, Dispenser and Family Chemist' on behalf of his widow Ellen as administrator and it is signed 'Received payment. F J Stringfellow pro Ellen Keetch.'

The debtor was Colonel S Williams, who may have been a doctor as the medical list was extensive, comprising thirty-two items such as Liniment, Corn Plaster, Prussic acid, Embrocation, Ammonia, Syrup, Laudenum, Camomile and 'Mixture 16360 for Negro Woman', giving a total cost from January to May of $16.20.

However, England's great topic in 1851 was not America but the forthcoming 'Great Exhibition of the Industries of All Nations' proposed by the Prince Consort 'to teach English Manufacturers that they might improve their own work by comparing it with and studying the work of Fellow Nations'. Hyde Park was the venue, and there, under the direction of Mr Paxton, head gardener to the Duke of Devonshire, a great Palace of iron and glass, four times the length of St Paul's Cathedral, was being constructed.

The completed Crystal Palace excited universal admiration because of its vastness and beauty united with a sense of lightness, symmetry and grace. Seventeen thousand exhibitors participated and when opened to the public by the Queen on the morning of 1 May the springtime sun shone brightly through the glass roof upon trees, flowers and banners. It seemed a fairyland. Undoubtedly John Stringfellow later went there to view the latest developments of science and the marvels of engineering, and his friend Arthur Hull also visited 'by excursion train only 12s 7d up and back, and this was cheap travelling'. By the time the Exhibition concluded on 15 October over 6 million people had viewed what had been the greatest show in history.

*   *   *

Although there is coincidence of timing, it was probably the anticipatory publicity and excitement preluding the Great Exhibition which had prompted John Stringfellow to re-contact Henson's notable helper John Chapman on 17 February after a lapse of some eight years: 'I have been endeavouring for some time past to find out your address, and trust I have at last succeeded. I have thought of doing something with the Aerial models this summer and wish to have your opinion about it. I have advanced several steps in the right way since I saw you last. Should this note come into the hands intended if you will acknowledge it I will give you further particulars in the matter.'

Chapman immediately wrote from his house at Paddington, London: 'It was with surprise as well as pleasure that I received this morning yours of yesterday; for I had heard that you went to California with Mr Marriott. I shall be glad to hear of any advance you are making with your aerial machines, and if any opinion or hint I can give will assist you I shall be so much the more gratified. It is some time since I paid any attention to the subject, and since I did so I have been anxiously occupied with other matters. But I suppose I can pretty readily rub up my recollections and go over the subject again.'

On receipt on 20 February, Stringfellow immediately outlined the scope of his continuing aeronautical work in following up his 1848 achievement of the world's first powered, heavier-than-air flight: 'Thank you for your prompt reply to my note — I am glad I have found you. Since I saw you I have made an entire new model Aerial Machine 12 feet in expanse of wing, very strong and manageable, far superior to anything done before, I think in every respect, and carries little over one fourth of a pound to the foot. It will consequently sustain itself at a much slower speed than any previous one, which is very desirable for exhibiting in a limited space. I have three models and I think in that state that something may be done with them.

'I wish to take your opinion as to the best method of proceeding — whether to exhibit them on my own account or throw myself into the hands of some parties such as the Polytechnic or Great Exhibition.

'The Public I know expect too much when they hear the high sounding words Aerial Steam Navigation, but I feel perfectly satisfied I can show the Scientific World that a Steam Engine can be made to fly. The new model after running 7 or 8 yards on a level wire has got into a sufficient speed to sustain itself and when liberated floats on very nicely any distance I have yet been able to try it. I have not tryed [sic] it in the open air but should do so before I brought it to Town. I have no doubt it will fly well on a still day as my propelling force is more than ample. Having, as well as yourself, devoted so much time and expense to this subject I think something ought to be made of it.'

That letter makes nonsense of the absent Frederick John's much quoted but uninformed later dismissal of the intervening years that 'This experimenter rested for a long time, satisfied with what he had effected.' It also invalidates conclusions limiting the extent of Stringfellow's work drawn by such reputable authors as Davy, Ballantyne and Pritchard, or the assumptions of Gibbs-Smith, for here are three or more models completed before the end of February 1851 whereas only the 1848 machine has previously been recorded.

Chapman replied with wise consideration: 'I scarcely know how to advise you on the subject mentioned in yours of yesterday. I can perhaps however say a few words which may caution if they do not assist you.

'My opinion would be altogether against putting the matter again into the hands of parties whose only interest would be that of a public show. As was very plain in both former attempts, these practised showmen have no just idea of the care, labour, time and money required by new mechanical affairs. All they want is something, sound or unsound, which will draw shillings from the public, and they are too impatient for the day when they begin to exhibit to know or care for the thing itself or for anything connected with it. If you were to make an agreement with any such man he would advertise the agreement next day and expect you to be ready by the day following; and if you did not fulfil all his ignorant and unfounded expectations and all his puffing assertions to the public, you would have a quarrel on your hands.

'The Polytechnic, which I believe is in highly respectable hands, is I think hardly the place for you. Its hall is I think neither long enough to do justice to the machine nor sufficiently clear for its flight. Besides they also, altho' much more reasonable than other parties, would look on it almost entirely as a show. I could obtain an introduction to Sir George Cayley its President if on consideration it be thought desirable.

'The rules of the Great Exhibition would prevent the Aerial Project's admission, besides which I hardly think it practicable to exhibit it there.

'I will think of the matter further. The only thing which at present offers to my thoughts is to lay the business before Mr Fox of the firm of Fox and Henderson the contractors for the Crystal Palace. If they would get a temporary building of sufficient dimensions say 24 feet wide and 400 feet long from the same

castings as the Palace, taking their chance of payment for the use
of it (at a high rate) out of the proceeds, and looking forward to a
profitable connection with the future prosecution of the invention
for use, possibly something might be done. Whether they would
listen to it I cannot guess; but perhaps the degree of confidence
Mr Fox has in me might be sufficient to induce him to consider it.
It is clear that they would do nothing about it on any such footing
until they were satisfied of the reality of the progress already
made and of the strong probability of eventual success for actual
use. They would therefore require statements to be vouched to
them and experiments which they could witness.

'If you think the above worth attempting I shall be ready to
open the business to Mr Fox in such manner as on reflection may
seem to me most likely to succeed. I fear he is at present too
much engaged with the Crystal Palace to be likely to give much
attention to a thing so romantic as this will at first appear to him
— a difficulty I will do my best to obviate if you wish.

'My other connections are so little accustomed to adventures
of this kind that I could hardly make any of them available at first,
altho' if wanted they might come in as the matter became intelli-
gible to them. Nor do I know whether there is a room sufficient
for your purpose in London, engaged or disengaged: that however may be learned by advertising.'

Stringfellow penned to him in his sloping hand on 22 February:
'I write a line in reply to yours received this morning. It contains
similar opinions to my own as regards the parties you are pleased
to call showmen. I should not like to join any unless of a scientific
turn who could appreciate the thing. I think it will be desirable to
proceed with caution — therefore it will perhaps be better for you
to have time to broach the subject to parties in such a manner as
you may think best and report progress when convenient. In the
meantime I will proceed to perfect every arrangement for experimenting. We have no room in Chard exceeding 20 yards and this
is much too short to show what I could wish. The Chinese Exhibition room I think the only place large enough in London is
already occupied.

'I should like to pursue the subject with that energy which I
think it deserves but I do not feel very sanguine as to forming a
connection for carrying the invention into useful application, not
but I consider it capable, but I am afraid the advantages are too
distant to be appreciated by the present generation. I should
much like to make the acquaintance of Sir George Cayley. I have
always considered him the father of Aerial Navigation and I know
his whole heart has been on the matter. He must now be getting
old, for it is some years since his first articles made their
appearance in the *Mechanics Magazine* on the subject and first

touched a chord in my visionary brain.'

An interval of six weeks ensued, then on 4 April he again wrote to Chapman: 'I am very anxious to know if you have made any further enquiries about The Aerial Project. I had hoped ere this to have been able to report some out-door experiments but the weather has been so very bad and the ground so wet that I found it impossible to do anything without damaging and soiling the models. There must be no mistake about the models flying before I bring them to the Metropolis. I consider the fact must be made notorious that they have made considerable flights out of doors before people will be satisfied with what they see in a room. The greatest difficulty I have to contend with is the want of a room sufficiently large to carry on my preparatory experiments which you know are more numerous than a person unacquainted with the subject would suppose.

'I should like to have a short lecture or two written on the subject and do not know any person so capable as yourself. Should it not interfere too much with your other engagements I should like you to take the matter in hand.

'I am now making an entire new model in quite a different form and arrangements from any heretofore attempted and I believe when anything is done on a large scale it will be after this plan. Hoping to hear from you shortly, I am etc.'

Chapman was busy writing a book entitled *The Cotton and Commerce of India* based on his unfortunate experiences between 1844 and 1850 in attempting to establish the proposed Great Indian Peninsular Railway, but he cautiously replied to Stringfellow on the 12th: 'I am sorry that your letter of the 4th has remained some days unanswered. This has happened partly through my having been unexpectedly very closely engaged with some heavy Indian affairs but chiefly through my being unable to see how I could effectually serve you until I could adduce the success of actual experiments against the incredulity with which any proposition founded on an aerial project is everywhere met. If I could hear of a place at all suitable for exhibiting your machine which could be had at small cost (comparatively small I mean) I would not hesitate to encourage you to engage it as soon as your new attempts shall shew that you are sufficiently advanced to use it to advantage. But I cannot find such a one, except perhaps by advertising, and even then it is extremely doubtful. If you wish it, I will advertise in *The Times*.

'Meanwhile I have applied to Fox & Henderson for an approximate estimate for a room on the Exhibition plan of 400 feet long by 24 wide. I expect this estimate every hour. I have also mentioned your machine to a gentleman not disinclined to engineering enterprize and have left on his mind an impression which may or may not be used to advantage as circumstance may hereafter determine.

'In judging of these matters it will be necessary to take into account how far you are prepared to bear the risk and expense of any proceedings yourself, and how far you will wish to associate others with you. I consider this letter only an instalment of the answer I wish to give you; but I am unwilling to delay it longer. If anything occurs to you from what I have said perhaps you will be so good as to state it that I may take it into account in any further effort.'

On 16 April, Stringfellow wrote: 'In reply to yours of last Saturday I do not think from enquiries I made when I was in London that there is a room sufficiently long to exhibit the models, with the exception of the Chinese exhibition room unless it is somewhere recently put up. The size of the place you are endeavouring to get an estimate of is not exactly the thing. Twenty-four feet is not wide enough. If 100 or 150 feet was taken off the ends and added to the sides it would answer the purpose much better; but I am afraid with my country notions the expense of creating such a place would almost frighten me.

'With regard to associating others in the matter, this will entirely depend upon what assistance they would render. I think any party ought to provide a good place in a good locality for exhibiting, on condition of receiving something like one third of the profits of each day's exhibition after deducting the current expenses. Should I not find parties liberal enough to take a risk something like this and I find it necessary to bear the whole expense and risk myself I should very likely do it in a more humble way. That is I should endeavour to take the premises somewhere in the neighbourhood of London where there would be sufficient room to erect a building suitable for the purpose which building I should put up as cheap as I could, partly of boards and part canvas. The greatest drawback I see to this way of proceeding would be its locality — too far from the centre of attraction. I don't know whether the preceding remarks are anything of what you wish me to say. Any questions you may wish to ask I will endeavour to reply to. Of course I should wish any parties to satisfy themselves with what I have done before they incur any risk whatever.'

Next day Chapman replied with great practicality: 'Your favour of the 16th has reached me. Messrs Fox & Henderson inform me that the building such as described would cost £1975. This sum of course might be diminished by shortening the building, or possibly also by making it a part of the agreement that they should take it again after a certain time, and by making a floor to only part of its length.

'My reason for saying only 24 feet wide was that is the width of one compartment of the Crystal Palace, so that no new patterns or plans of any sort would be required. The length 400 feet, seemed to me desirable in order that it might be shewn in a manner to satisfy scrupulous scientific investigation that the machine performed a real flight — that is, that it kept up its velocity through so great a distance by means of the power it carried and was not merely shown as flying by means of velocity given to it at starting. The greater the length through which this could be done, the better. It may be reckoned as quite certain that the moment so novel and ambitious machine has any apparent success its credit will be assailed by objections from quarters of established reputation which it will be quite necessary to repel by measurable facts. A short building, even a moderately long one, will hardly give room for demonstrating those facts. I took however the particular length of 400 feet only for the sake of a figure; but the estimate founded on it will give a good guess for any other length.

'Considered as an exhibition to be made to pay, some degree of handsomeness in the building would contribute to its success — so much is the world led by appearances, and by those whom it might be difficult to get to resort to a place without appearance. The thinkers and workers of course would go anywhere, but they are not enough to make up a paying audience. On the other hand it must be said that too costly a building might run away with the largest possible profits, and would at any rate involve some risk.

'If you are far enough advanced to afford satisfaction, by experiment, of your mechanical success I should think it would not be difficult to find persons willing to join in the risk of expenses of exhibition; but then those persons must have a voice in the manner in which their money is to be laid out — and if they thought an eligible though expensive building would be most likely to succeed in realizing a profit I suppose you would hardly object to their views in that matter if you retained under your own control everything relating to the machine itself.

'If on the other hand you wish to make your attempt on a plan which permits you to be more independent, and will tell me of what dimensions and construction you would wish the building to be, I will try to procure for you any information as to cost, site etc which you may need.'

To that the inventive John Stringfellow responded on 23 April with a futuristic idea that was revived sixty years later as the canvas Bessoneaux hangar and the later pneumatic Handley Page shed: 'I was at Tiverton when your letter reached me or I should have replied sooner. The estimate from Fox & Henderson seems a large sum to be expended for appearances sake; this is one of the reasons which makes me think I ought to connect myself with parties that understand these matters better than I do. I don't object to the length of 400 feet, the longer the better, but it ought to be of a proportionate height and width. Twenty-four feet is much too narrow for that length and does not give sufficient room for any deviation in the flight of the model, nor is there side room enough for an audience.

'Do you not think something very elegant in the shape of a tent could be fitted up for less money: an Aerial tent or Palace made of canvas or calico rendered impervious to air and to be filled and kept up by a blowing machine so that no timber would be required to support it, being firmly secured on all sides to the ground? This might be embellished by transparent paintings of appropriate subjects from the flight of Elijah to all real and imaginary projects down to the present time. This may be going too far, but there is some novelty in the idea. However, as you observe, any parties engaged in the matter would in a measure decide what would be the best kind of a building.

'We had a lovely almost a summer day here last Saturday. I had hoped the weather had cleared up so that I may try some decisive experiments and be able to report something worth hearing, but the weather is again cold and wet.

'In the new model I am making I arrange my machinery much better than any heretofore and have dispensed with all cog wheels and gearing of that kind, and the engine and propellers seem to work right well and cannot get out of order. I should like to alter the other machines to the same plan but I begin to feel very anxious as the season is fast approaching.

'With regard to any parties that would like to engage in the matter, I suppose they would like to see experiments somewhere. We have but one room in the town 20 yards long, but I have some thought of constructing a temporary place in my own garden nearly 40 yards in length. Do you think this would be sufficiently large to show anything they would be satisfied with, or what other arrangements would be required before anything decisive can be entered into? I feel myself I ought to have some successful outdoor experiments.'

Tantalisingly no further correspondence of this period has been located, nor any account of indoor trials witnessed by the public, and yet Stringfellow was unlikely to have left those four or possibly five models as static exhibits when there was a large secluded meadow adjacent to his garden and the weather must sometimes have been dead calm.

The story of his achievements remains largely shrouded because he was so modestly unassuming. Though Stringfellow made a few notes on engine and boiler data such experimenters rarely make full written record of day to day successes and disasters but quietly proceed with their labours, considering cause and effect, scrapping what they have made in favour of a modified project, and again and again. In later years John Stringfellow continued to refer to his models as though there were a number. Certainly he long maintained 'premises in which I carried out my experiments'. Analytical inspection of the batch of photographs of his stored models taken many years later when large bellows-type cameras were in vogue show sufficient components such as cabins, sets of wings, tails, propellers and mountings, boilers and engines, to indicate that half a dozen machines may have been built by him. Of these, he considered that a large 'bat-wing' model was the most successful, and this must be the 12ft model to which he referred in his second letter to Chapman. It had greater area and lower aspect ratio than previously and the twin four-bladed propellers were now inset at the centre of the wing chord instead of at the trailing edge. It must have been tried at least in hand-launched flight because even in a letter written 15 years later to Brearey, Stringfellow said: 'I consider it more perfect than the one I had at Cremorne,' yet he adds: 'I was not able to try it for want of a room.' But at 68 one makes dyslectic mistakes in writing, so he probably meant not able to try it 'fully for want of room'.

*   *   *

In that same month of September 1852 in which the great Duke of Wellington died, Stringfellow must have read with interest in the current *Mechanics Magazine* an article by seventy-nine year-old Sir George Cayley on 'Governable Parachutes', revealing that he had recently experimented with a glider which had three almost square superimposed wings, each of just over 100 sq ft area, and 'after the balance and steerage was ascertained, a boy of about ten years of age was floated off the ground for several yards.' That would eventually be followed by a monoplane version in the form of a low aspect ratio kite-like wing of 500 square feet intended as a man carrier to be launched from a balloon.

Meanwhile Stringfellow had become more practically involved with electrical work, and on 2 October 1852 he applied for a Provisional Patent for 'Galvanic batteries' for medical use. As the result of experiments he had developed plates of zinc bound with insulating material and enclosed by a perforated copper sheet soldered along the adjoining edges. A number of these small elements, proportioned to the intensity of the current required, were connected together and folded so that they could be inserted in a cover 'no larger than a lady's card case'. Wires passing through the top of the case carried discs or electrodes which could be attached to any part of the body, and the battery was energised by wiping the plates with a weak solution of acid as the active electrolite. Here was the fore-runner of modern electrical shock therapy.

The patent was granted on 5 January 1853, and there was immediate interest, for it was widely acclaimed by eminent medical practitioners, and the *Lancet* of 5 March and 2 July gave Stringfellow considerable praise for his invention. Advertisements in the Chard press stated that batteries could be bought in various sizes at a cost of 6s, 10s, 16s, 21s, and 31s 6d direct from John Stringfellow at Chard 'or from any respectable chemist'.

To ensure proper understanding he wrote a booklet of explanation entitled *Electricity and Galvanism in Relation to the Treatment of Disease.*

Promptly on 17 January the great Andrew Cross wrote a congratulatory letter: 'I have carefully examined your electrode-Voltaire pocket battery and am very much pleased with its scientific arrangements, its exceeding neatness and portability rendering it most admirably adapted for a variety of purposes, and particularly for medical uses for which purpose it is far superior to any I know. Its decomposing power considerably exceeds what might be expected from a combination of plates of so small a size and so comparatively few in number, and in its power is much more durable than I should have conceived. It is moreover readily channelled and easily kept in order and altogether displays great ingenuity in its construction. I am, in the meantime, my dear Sir, Yours very sincerely.'

The pages of history were slowly turning. Many outside events were making impact, and now England was drifting into war following a dispute between Russia and Turkey in which the Czar claimed the right to protect all Christian subjects in countries under Turkish rule bordering the Danube. England, France, Austria and Prussia agreed at a conference in Vienna to demand that the Sultan accede to the claim, but he refused and Russia declared war on Turkey. England and France rejected the Czar's proposal for an alliance and in March 1854 sent troops to Varne, in the Black Sea, causing the Russians to withdraw to their great naval arsenal of Sebastopol in the Crimea.

That summer Stringfellow's twenty-two year-old son Frederick John, excited by the stories of gold found in the Rio Grande, took ship from his American home at Galveston and worked passage to England in high hope of persuading his father to join in a mining venture proffering quick riches, but family tradition has it that his mother again feigned illness to ensure that her husband stayed at home.

The only established evidence that Fred had visited is a letter dated 10 May 1903, written when he was 71 to his friend C H M Alderson: 'In September 1854 I again went to Texas, but before leaving my father's house I copied from the walls of a large room (into a book) all particulars as to weight, speed, surface etc., of the various birds whose skins were nailed to the walls, and I collected all the papers relating to the experiments — which I am sorry to tell you I could not find when I next returned to England in '59 or '60.'

That same month of Frederick John's visit, John Chapman, who had so greatly assisted Henson and Stringfellow died at the age of 53, victim of a cholera epidemic which in London alone claimed 10,000 lives. He had become widely known as the promoter of the great Peninsular Railway, his mathematical and mechanical achievements were remarkable, and his books on India and its constitutional reform, plans for cotton production and for irrigation, were very highly regarded; he was equally famed as a political writer and gained the intellectual support of Cobden, Bright, Macauley and Sir Charles Napier.

Meanwhile there was the siege of Sebastopol, the great battles of Balaclava and Inkerman, and in this terrible winter of 1854, in which the troops suffered appallingly from lack of shelter and food, came the public re-appearance of the same Mr Roebuck who had introduced Henson's petition to the House of Commons and now as the result of public outcry, brought forward a motion in the House to enquire into the cause of mismanagement in the Crimea. This was passed by the Commons, forcing the Prime Minister, Lord Aberdeen, to resign, and he was succeeded by Lord Palmerston in 1855.

Not until March 1856 was a Peace Treaty signed by Russia in Paris with undertaking not to refortify Sebastopol nor keep a fleet in the Black Sea; but for Britain, peace was short lived because mutiny in India broke out in the following January, stirred by rumour that the British intended to introduce Christianity by force.

That spring of 1857 also saw the wedding of Frederick John Stringfellow, now 25 and established not only as a chemist but was also practising dentistry. His bride was a young English girl, Emma Jane Weston Higgs, an orphan who had emigrated to Texas from Hereford with her uncle and aunt, Mr & Mrs David Richardson, relatives of W Richardson the owner and publisher of the *Galveston News,* and she also had an uncle, Thomas J Higgs, the local grocer. Her home was at a nearby fruit farm notable for an avenue of pomegranates. She and Fred had known each other for some years and enjoyed considerable mutual social activity, evidenced by a surviving invitation of 22 February 1853 for the Galveston Artillery's Fourth Annual Assembly at Tremont House and one on 8 February 1856 to a Ball organised by the local Freemasons of which Frederick John had become a member, and many such invitations followed in succeeding years. There were also records extant of various friends such as Mott J Love, W Baulard, John Sealy, Dr E Randall, and the Rev Benjamin Enton of the Anglical Congregation.

The young couple's marriage licence states:

> This is to certify that I, Jacob E. Rump, a Justice of the Peace in and for the said County of Galveston duly commissioned and qualified, on this first day of May A.D. One thousand Eight Hundred and Fifty Seven, celebrated the rights of matrimony between Fred. J. Stringfellow and Miss Emma Higgs according to law and pursuant to a marriage licence issued on the first day of May 1857 by Oscar Tarish, Clerk of the County Court of Galveston County.

Frederick John celebrated the occasion by writing a poem entitled 'The Wedding' which unfortunately was lost through loan to one of the several investigators of Stringfellow history, but a shipping 'Bill of Lading' dated August 1858 survives showing that a box 'contents unknown' was freighted to Emma Stringfellow in Galveston by the Barque *W H Wharton* sailing from Liverpool, and that the cost of 7s 6d had been paid in full. Frederick and Emma eventually had 15 children, three of whom were born in Galveston — the twins Laura and Clara, and Stella Texanna.

Coincidentally in the year of Fred's marriage, Sir George Cayley died on 15 December just before his eighty-fourth birthday, having achieved a final 'governable parachute' in 1853 which in the form of a monoplane briefly lifted his coachman for a short glide across a shallow vale on his Brompton estate in Yorkshire; but though there were now a few incipient designs of powered machines, none had flown, the nearest to achieving Stringfellow's success being a French naval officer, Felix du Temple who was alleged to have emulated him in 1857 with a successful but cruder model monoplane powered with a multi-blade propeller driven by steam engine.

*   *   *

Meanwhile the Indian Mutiny ran its course with the massacre of Cawnpore, recapture of Delhi, and the relief of Lucknow ending the rebellion, whereupon the British Government transferred the power and authority of the East India Company to the Crown and in 1858 the Queen was proclaimed Sovereign of India. The monopoly of the Hudson Bay Company was similarly terminated and its vast territory was converted into a British colony. Topically, people in England were more interested in the old question of Parliamentary Reform, but in the following year a new Bill extending everyone's right to a vote was defeated, and the new Prime Minister, Lord Derby, announced that in view of the domestic interests of the country and the grave condition of European affairs he recommended early dissolution of Parliament by Her Majesty, who again called upon Lord Palmerston to form an administration.

General Napoleon Bonaparte saw the international disarray as opportunity for further conquests, and on 3 May 1859 demanded that Austria must rule only as far as the Alps, leaving Italy free to the Adriatic shores. Inevitably a war of liberation ensued. In the north the combined forces of France and Sardinia defeated the Austrians and expelled them from Lombardy. In the south Garibaldi, a distinguished patriot and soldier, liberated Sicily and Naples, whereupon they joined Sardinia whose King, Victor Emanuel, was proclaimed King of Italy. Meanwhile fear of a French invasion of England led to formation of large bodies of volunteers as a permanent part of our regular army, and they took as their motto 'Defence not Defiance'. Perhaps it was that which engendered John Stringfellow's awakening interest in weapons of war — but it was the new art of photography to which he became increasingly devoted, for the uncertain process of the previous decade had been replaced by Scott-Archer's glass 'wet-plate' invention of 1851 giving printable negatives.

For some time Stringfellow had been practising this method with such success that he adopted the new art professionally. The *Chard Illustrated Magazine* of August 1859 carried a full page advertisement introducing his new photographic portrait establishment in High Street, Chard, with news that 'By a recent discovery, portraits can now be taken and transmitted through the post to any part of the world, without the possibility of breaking, and without extra charge'. Ten years later the weekly *Chronicle and Advertiser for Somerset, Dorset and Devon* was still carrying his advertisements. A large number of his photographic portraits are now held by John's great grand-daughter, and the Somerset Archaeological and Natural History Society has negatives of more at Taunton Castle.

Stringfellow's old idol, Richard Cobden, of the Anti-corn law days, was again in the news at the beginning of 1860 for his successful negotiation of a commercial treaty 'permitting English goods into France at low duties, and French wines and other goods to be admitted to England in the same way'. Whether Stringfellow was a wine drinker has escaped the record. More likely he was a beer drinker, for his great friend was William Tucker Toms, the brewer of High Street, among the close-knit group of industrialists and businessmen of Chard who frequently met and entertained each other in the slow tempo of those days. Certainly there was cause for celebration by the Stringfellows that summer, for the low transatlantic fare permitted Frederick John to visit them again, probably with Emma — though there are no details of the occasion other than that letter to Alderson forty-three years later in which he is uncertain whether he came in 1859 or 1860.

However, all was far from well in the conglomeration of territories which formed the great American Union, for there was deepening and ominous contention between the North and South part of that country over the employment of black Africans as slaves. When the country first achieved independence all provinces had held slaves, but they had later become illegal in the North where increasing emigration from Europe supplied sufficient labour for their industries. The South, however, was still dependent on slaves for economic production of cotton exports representing nearly 60 per cent of all American sales abroad. Without slave labour this great market would collapse. Consequently there was bitter feeling between Northern abolitionists and the slave States, which came to a head when Abraham Lincoln was nominated Republican candidate in the Presidential election, for the South was convinced that if he won it would lead to establishment of more new abolitionist States in the west.

As a first consequence the people of South Carolina, which had been the most restive under the Fugitive Slave Law, met in convention in Colombia and on 20 December 1860 voted their State out of the Union. On 9 January 1861 Mississippi followed suit, then Florida, Louisiana, and Texas. On 1 February the rebelling Confederated States of America was formed, of which Jefferson Davies became President on the ninth. Lincoln was inaugurated as President of the Union on 4 March.

Both sides swiftly armed. War opened with the Confederates spectacularly bombarding Fort Sumpter near the mouth of Charleston Harbour, Carolina on 13 April. Two days later Lincoln called out the militia of all loyal States to form an army of 75,000 men to put down 'combinations too powerful to be suppressed by the ordinary course of judicial proceedings'. On the nineteenth he declared the ports of all seceding States to be in a state of blockade.

To safeguard British shipping the British Government on 14 May published a 'Proclamation of Neutrality' in *The London Gazette*. Nevertheless British vessels going to Charleston for cotton or taking hardware to New Orleans were liable to seizure because of the swiftly intensifying state of war. So when on 7 July the English mail steamer *Trent* sailed from nearby Orleans via Havana for Southampton and was stopped with a shot across her bows from a Federal vessel, forcing the surrender of two Confederation Envoys, Frederick John Stringfellow decided to close down the Galveston business and endeavour to emigrate to England with his family, for it was apparent that if the blockade continued for several years it would bankrupt the Galveston trade. Meanwhile mail to and from Britain was seriously disrupted, but in mid-December came news via the new technical achievement of a cross-Atlantic undersea Telegraph cable that the Prince Consort had died following a feverish cold.

Chapter 8
The Great Exhibition

Of John Stringfellow's concurrent activities in Chard there is no specific record, but undoubtedly his photographic venture was attracting considerable attention for people loved 'having their picture taken', and there is evidence that his 21 year-old son Allan Harrison had also become proficient in this skill and was attending the shop full-time.

News of the American Civil War remained sketchy and disquieting. By April 1862 the Confederate forces were on the defensive, and even New Orleans at the mouth of the Mississippi had been lost with the great river valley about to follow, thus splitting the confederacy. Nevertheless the South had tremendous vitality, and on 30 August their General-in-Chief Robert E Lee won a notable victory at the second battle of Manassas in the wide vale of the Bull Run River beneath the mountains of that name; yet by the middle of October the counter-offensives of the Confederacy had been beaten back and the danger of Federal defeat in the North had passed, but fighting in the South continued for four years.

The tide of sanguinary conflict along the whole American frontier from west of Missouri to the shores of Virginia was deeply disturbing to the mind of Britain, and was having a bad impact on the Lancashire cotton industry, but for thirty year-old Frederick John Stringfellow in Galveston there had been an opportunity to run the gauntlet of the blockade and attempt the long sea voyage back to England, for his grandmother Keetch had recently died, so there were now no ties to keep him in Texas.

Exactly when, by which ship and what route he and his wife with their only surviving daughter, Stella Texanna, returned to England is not known, but in 1863 he and his family were living at Ide, near Exeter, where a fourth daughter, Maud, was born on 12 November. Not long afterwards he set up as a dentist at Candle Cottage, East Street, in the quiet country town of Crewkerne some eight miles from Chard, for by now he had become particularly skilled at that art in Galveston and his business as a chemist had afforded valuable insight into the use of anaesthetics — in fact he was the first in the Wessex area to offer 'painless extraction'. His rival was an ostler in Crewkerne named Nat Gould who had a handy pair of horse forceps for pulling horses' teeth, but used it on humans as a side line. Two farm workers from nearby Merriott were heard to say: 'What! Go down there and pay one shilling to Mr Stringfellow? You go to Nat Gould and be pulled all over the house for fourpence!'

At that time Dr Hunt of Yeovil and Frederick Stringfellow at Crewkerne were the only two dentists between Exeter and Salisbury — a distance spanned by the London and South West Railway which had recently opened a line between those two cities, and in 1860 had at last established a station three miles south of Chard. Then when a local branch line to Crewkerne, Beaminster, Axminster and Seaton was opened in 1863 Frederick John not only was able to hold a twice monthly surgery at his father's house in Chard but also a day's attendance each month at these places, though it is said that at Seaton, where he soon added a second day, he much preferred to sit on the beach and watch the seagulls flying. This was a subject he must often have discussed with his father who regularly visited Candle Cottage to see his grandchildren, who in the course of time would tell their children how they remembered him sitting there, and of the tricks with electricity with which he amused them.

As a keen gardener John must also have discussed that quiet hobby with his dentist son who had found great pleasure in the flowers that the warm abundance of the American South had afforded, and at Crewkerne he gained early notoriety as the introducer of white begonias as well as exotic insect-eating flowers from Texas standing in pots on sloping racks in his greenhouse for easier inspection. His interests also extended to keeping parakeets and doves, and as a Texan Freemason he was welcomed as a member of the Parrett and Axe Masonic Lodge No. 184 at Crewkerne, later receiving provincial honours and eventually becoming Grandmaster.

*   *   *

Meanwhile the Civil War in America had cut off supplies of cotton in 1863, resulting in great distress among the textile operatives of Lancashire, for whom the nation raised £1 million for a Relief Fund; nevertheless general industrial trade was widely prospering, particularly the sales of arms and munitions in immense quantities to both the Union and Confederacy. Certainly England at this time was more interested in the regeneration of Poland from its despotic yoke of Russia than interfering with the profitable American Civil War, and concurrently was casting a prospecting eye at the possibilities of the unexplored central lands of Africa.

The course of peaceful industry and the accumulation of wealth proceeded undisturbed in the following year, and the gradual abatement of distress in Lancashire diffused into a general feeling of relief and satisfaction. There was even a national move to mark the 300th anniversary of Shakespeare's birth with a Pavilion erected at Stratford-upon-Avon by public subscription, and in London it was resolved to plant an oak in his honour at the foot of Primrose Hill. Even the Chard Institution, which John String-fellow had helped found 25 years earlier, paid due homage. But in America that other English speaking nation was still engaged in a bitter fight, so Frederick John Stringfellow had long abandoned all hope of returning there. Yet 1865 at last brought an end to the war with capitulation of the Confederate Army of Virginia, and Lee's surrender to the Union's General Grant at the McLean Court House, Appomattox. But even while the Northern states were celebrating the conclusion of that bitter dispute, in which each side lost some 275,000 men, their great President, Abraham Lincoln, was assassinated on 14 April at Ford's Theatre, Washington.

Many years later it transpired that during the Civil War, Stringfellow's erstwhile partner Henson devised a big breech-loading iron gun 'the theory being that the breech forms the entire resisting medium behind the powder in the barrel'. It had been offered to the Union Government, but Gideon Welles, the Secretary of the Navy, turned it down on the grounds that 'practical results are not in favour of breech-loading cannon, nor has there been anything elicited so far in gun making that would justify accepting it'. Unknown to Stringfellow, Henson was still pursuing his inventive way.

But now 1866 brought war in Europe occasioned by Austria and Germany over-running Denmark's provinces of Schleswig and Holstein, and then heading towards war between themselves. France and Italy were drawn into the net, and in June diplomatic relations between Austria and Prussia were suspended. Within three days war began, resulting in the collapse of Austria two months later.

The beginning of the year had also introduced another landmark in the history of man's attempt at aerial navigation, for on 12 January the Aeronautical Society of Great Britain was founded by six people at Argyll House, Camden Hill, London under chairmanship of the 8th Duke of Argyll. They were James Glaisher the balloonist and founder member of the Meteorological Society, Francis Wenham, a curly bearded naval architect who had built an unsuccessful small quintuple-winged man-lifting glider, Dr Diamond, whose activities are not recorded, James Butler, a wealthy balloonist and bearded, 40 year-old Frederick Brearey, a friend of Glaisher's who was fascinated by the possibilities of flying, and now undertook the responsibilities of Secretaryship of the Committee.

The Duke of Argyll had been one of Cayley's friends, was author of *The Reign of Law* dealing with the structure of the universe, and was convinced that heavier than air devices would be the real flying machines. But it was Glaisher who was the Council's tower of strength. His knowledge of the atmosphere and weather was outstanding, for he had established over 50 meteorological stations using the most up-to-date instruments, but he was also an astronomer of great ability. Speaking at the Society's opening meeting, he concentrated on the importance of knowledge of atmospheric currents, but apparently had never heard of John Stringfellow or Cayley, for he said: 'When we consider that the act of flying is purely a mechanical action it seems remarkable that no correct demonstration has ever been given of the combined principles upon which flight is performed, nor of the absolute force required to maintain such flight.'

The Society proved of immediate though limited interest, and on 1 June Wenham wrote to the *Mechanics Magazine*: 'I may state that the function of the Aeronautical Society has developed the fact, by communications received, that many are now of the opinion that man may yet command the air as a medium of transport in any direction,' and on 27 June he inaugurated public lectures at the Society with a classic paper *On Aerial Locomotion*, during which he mentioned: 'It seems remarkable that Sir George Cayley, on finding that at high speeds and very oblique incidences the supporting effect became transferred to the front edge, the idea should not have occurred to him that a narrow plane with its long edge in the direction of motion would have been equally effective.' But that was what Stringfellow and Henson had long ago discovered was the most efficient form of wing in their invention of the aeroplane.

In 1867 open meetings were chaired by Wenham in April and July. Because few scientists could be persuaded to believe in the aeroplane it was difficult to keep the Society viable despite the enthusiasm of the few. To obtain wider publicity Brearey proposed at the August Council Meeting that an exhibition of machinery and miscellaneous items connected with aeronautics should be organised and at the next meeting the Council ambitiously agreed that it should be held the following year at the rebuilt Crystal Palace at Sydenham. The only question was: were there sufficient potential exhibits to fill that huge hall?

Brearey had already heard of the local fame of Chard's 'flying man' John Stringfellow, and earlier had sent him the Society's Annual Report for information on its activities. On 14 October he wrote to him with typical Victorian formality: 'I enclose for you a circular of our proposed Exhibition as I hear you might perhaps have something to exhibit. Perhaps you might be able to furnish me with a few names of such as take an interest in the subject.'

Stringfellow's instructive response can be inferred from Brearey's next letter of 21 November: 'I was very glad to receive your letter this morning. I quite agree that if you have succeeded in making a flying model you have solved a problem under discouraging circumstances. The next thing is to convince the world of it and no better opportunity exists for attracting general attention than the coming Exhibition. I wish you could give me a full description of the performance of your model. I think I would publish it in our next Annual Report now compiling.'

Four days later Stringfellow replied: 'The principle I have been working on is very simple. I have adhered to the Bird as near as possible, merely substituting the screw wheel as the propeller or driver, keeping the wings rigid as a sustaining surface. I hope to look up some of my things and try if I can put a Model in something like ship-shape, but unfortunately I have not sufficient length of barn to experiment in, having let the Premises in which I formerly carried on my experiments.

'I have often thought that they might have got up a working Model at the Crystal Palace that would have attracted some attention without very much expense, but small working models require to be made very nice. All the flights have been made in a long room's still atmosphere. Perhaps something might be done in large Models by shortening the wings and placing one tier a little distance above the other. Still it would have its drawbacks and be of no assistance I think in small Models. I will try and send you a photo of the Models or parts as soon as I can manage to do so.'

Perhaps it was too much of a task at 68 years old to give the full description of flight performance that Brearey needed, but he began reassembling one or more models, somewhat damaged though they were after 20 years storage, and took several photographs, but these cannot be positively identified.

On 18 December Brearey wrote: 'I am very much obliged for your interesting letter and photos which I shall read and show at our Council meeting on Thursday. It is a great pity that experience like yours should be lost to the world, but I think that you see that the time has arrived when publicity may be given to your attempts. So far as I can see you would secure the prize to be given for the best working Model, always supposing that it would maintain flight for the distance you state of 40 or 50 yards. I have yet to examine more closely with a magnifier your photos. At present I do not see how you get your motive power. Does the machine carry its own motor?

'Mr Artingstall is getting up his "pipe experiment" details in the Society's Report in a letter signed FDA. The rapid wing motion evidently raised and poised his model in the air, but your propeller is doubtless more under control and in less compass. In a large machine the wafting wings would be beyond control.

'You must send me a "Paper" for our next general meeting in February. The Exhibition will take place the latter end of May or beginning of June, which I trust will give you time to compete, and if we Exhibit at the Crystal Palace there will be ample space and room to see.

'The Shipwrecked Mariners Society have awarded £50 for a prize for the best form of Kite for enabling a communication from a wreck on shore, or between two vessels at sea. Perhaps you may have thought of this yourself?'

That last paragraph must have stimulated Stringfellow's imagination, for the legend has been handed down through three generations of his descendants that he built a great kite, but no details have been discovered. Nor is his reply to Brearey extant, but he evidently proposed to exhibit one or more of his small engines at the Exhibition, and instead of sending the 1847 model, decided he could now build a better machine incorporating Cayley's pioneering advice of using super-posed wings, for that had been endorsed by Francis Wenham after trying the system with his compact little 16-foot multi-wing glider. It was not the structural advantage that had appealed to Wenham but easier launching whereby 'the aeroplanes could be raised in sequence, like a super-posed series of kites so the first would carry the weight of the machine itself, and the next would lift that of the body.'

Stringfellow envisaged a model triplane of ⅓ hp, but instead of his former penchant for a tapering wing outline he used simpler rectangular wings foreshadowing the strutted box-like wire-braced structure of eventual early 20th century aeroplanes. He stuck to his twin-propeller arrangement but instead of using crossed cord drive from a pulley on the crankshaft he reverted to long connecting rods working in opposite directions from the double acting piston rod of the engine. The relative spans of the wings were approximately 8 ft, 7 ft, and 6 ft — described as '21 ft frontage'.

There were potential rivals in the offing, so on 30 December Brearey warned: 'I had the pleasure to read your last letter to the Council which afforded much gratification. One of the members asked for your address but I think that you had better not correspond with him as he is himself a Patentee of a flying machine, and I hope he has had more delicacy than his intention implied.'

*   *   *

The year 1867 for Stringfellow had been largely redeemed by this revived interest in the possibility of aerial navigation, for England had been passing through a turbulent time. There had been more trouble from the Irish with outrages and murder in Manchester and London, and all across the country there were strikes initiated by trade unions, among whom the London Taylors' Union was indicted at the Central Criminal Court as a warning to others against misdemeanour of 'conspiring together in restraint of trade and the freedom of personal actions'.

However there were no disturbances at Chard. From earliest days of the lace industry every effort had been made to prevent their workers from joining a trade union, and every new apprentice had to sign an undertaking not to join such a union or pay anything towards its support directly or indirectly. Consequently the lace factories were flourishing to the benefit of all Chard and John Stringfellow's several businesses were still surviving, whether engineering, photography or electrical treatment, and the practice of his son, Frederick John as a surgeon-dentist had considerably extended because of his use of anaesthetics, though as an alternative: 'Mr Stringfellow called attention to his vulcanite base for artificial teeth by the use of which the necessity of extracting all stumps was obviated.'

He also offered help for his father's new projects, as the old man in his sixty-ninth year was beginning to feel frail, and correspondence with Brearey was taking much time. Writing to him on 1 April 1868, John Stringfellow explained: 'I must apologise for not thanking you earlier for the Report. It is quite refreshing to look over Mr Wenham's remarks. I am afraid I could not donate you a Paper worth reading. I had commenced one intending to give you some little account of my former experiments but am so bad with rheumatics in my head that I am obliged to give it up. I have been troubled with it all winter and instead of having the theme in my head it is more like a railway train passing through.

'I am getting on very slowly with the Model but I think tolerable satisfactory and hope I shall have it finished in time. How do you propose to test the light engine? By drawing a weight over the pulley? I have one that I made for a larger Model very light in proportion to its power. I am afraid I shall not have time to arrange it for testing as I must finish the new Model first.'

The reference to 'larger model' may refer either to the bat wing or the larger pair of stacked wings revealed in several photographs.

His letter continues with the old plaint: 'One great difficulty I have to contend with is the want of a room sufficiently large to try the Model as there are a number of little matters that would require to be nicely adjusted before it could possibly be balanced nicely on the wing. I want thoroughly to test the power of the steam engine to carry the Model before I brought it up as I have made considerable deviation from my former arrangement.

'The Model when completed will be about 12 lbs in weight, water, fuel and all, and will work about 10 minutes. Lineal frontage of sustaining planes 21 feet. Superficial area of sustaining planes about 30 feet. Sectional area of the entire machine about 177 inches, and all angles are reduced as much as possible. Two propellers 21 inches diameter, the blades of which can be regulated to any angle. I shall have no difficulty to work the propellers I should think at over 400 revolutions per minute, of course depending on the angle they are set.'

On 10 April Brearey replied: 'I am indeed very sorry to hear of your rheumatic sufferings. It is hard to exercise thought and ingenuity in the midst of pain. I sent your letter to Mr Wenham to hear what he said about the matter proposed to test the engines. He says this question has got to be considered.

'If your model should succeed and achieve flight I suppose you would like to exhibit it yourself at the Palace, and I further think that if you applied, the Society might pay your expenses. After our nine days I think the Crystal Palace Company would make an engagement with you for as long as the Exhibition remained open, for we shall lease it to them afterwards.'

Brearey followed that up on 19 May with information that the Crystal Palace Company had modified the conditions for their prize from flight duration of 20 minutes to five, and had increased the prize for light engines to £5.

Three days later Stringfellow replied: 'What I am aiming at is to show the possibility of making a steam engine fly — but you must not expect too much from me as I am labouring under great disadvantages, particularly as regards home. I have kept the Model as small as I possibly could, but the principal is capable of extension and would be better on a larger scale.

'I have had my attention drawn to some reports in the newspapers of startling disclosures made at the last meeting of the Society, but have not seen anything from which I can draw inference of its nature, though trust they are in the right direction.'

That referred to the official report of the first meeting of the Society that year on 25 March when Wenham in the course of a discussion on a paper by A Alexander stated that: 'Within the last few weeks Mr Charles Spencer has succeeded in taking short flights of a hundred feet from level ground in a machine of his own invention and construction and entirely by muscular force. I look upon its achievement as something more than the first steps of infancy, for it has overcome what to me has been an almost insuperable difficulty in that of making the first start.' The device comprised a dart-shaped wing of 140 square feet to which was attached a pair of waftable wings of 15 square feet with which the inventor proposed to propel the machine after starting with a preliminary run down hill.

Unaware of these details John Stringfellow continued his letter: 'Since writing the above I have received your note. I think the alteration made in the Crystal Palace prize was very desirable. Where would a machine be in 20 minutes!

'I have a working steam engine which I used in one of my Aerial Models, very light and efficient. The boiler contains near upon 4 feet of effective heating surface when charged with 2 quarts of water. I can raise the steam to 100 pounds pressure in 3 minutes with liquid fuel. The cylinder is two inch diameter with a three inch stroke. Weight of boiler and fireplace 8¼ lbs; cylinder with connecting rods etcetera 3¾ lbs; altogether about 12 lbs without supply of water. Will work well for near ten minutes keeping good dry working steam from 60 to 100 lbs pressure. Do you think it would be worth bringing up? Of course I have taken it out of the old Model. Should have arranged it in the same working frame but shall not have time.'

That reference to the 'old Model' may mean the original *Ariel* model, judging by the weight. Stringfellow again continues: 'I do not know how you purpose judging the capabilities of a light engine. I have two small engines as light as anything that have been made according to the power. Still in this I may have been mistaken as I am perfectly ignorant of what others have done. I do not see that any description is necessary in the catalogue beyond "Aerial steam carriage light steam engines". I have forwarded you a rough description of the new Model for your satisfaction, but should not like it to be put in the catalogue. I have a great objection to public exhibitions or saying anything to cause public expectation which may not be realised.

'The balloons will please the public, but mechanical flying is a different thing, at least at present, and if we escape without making ourselves ridiculous in the eyes of the public we must be thankful. Treat the flying man Spencer kindly. He is beginning at the right end. This is how the goose learns to fly. His experiments are on the true principle and I don't see any reason why the art of flying may not be taught as a branch in the art of gymnastics.

'I don't want to trespass on the funds of the Society much, but can't afford to be away from home on expenses. I have already spent a great deal of time on the matter.'

Typical of Stringfellow was the penultimate paragraph revealing his life-long modesty and reluctance to claim any particular merit in his pioneering successes. Much of the detail is consequently lost to history.

Concurrently on 23 May Brearey acknowledged Stringfellow's earlier letter, telling him: 'I am truly sorry to hear of your continued indispostion. It is depressing to be obliged to contemplate the end of labours which promised so much for the advancement of the Science which has at last become acknowledged as such. So far as I am able I am anxious to preserve to posterity the remembrance of the labours and achievements of all those who have given their attention throughout life to the elucidation of the principles of flight. One day a history must be written, and if you possess a photograph of yourself I should like a copy.'

That was followed on 28 May with a letter saying: 'Thank you for the photo. After the Exhibition the Aeronautical Society will take an extraordinary start so that we may look forward to something more extensive next year. I presume I shall have the description for the catalogue on 1 June.

'I do not gather from your letter what is the capacity and capability of the engine and boiler attached to the Model you are making, but only of the engine and boiler you have detached from your old Model, which I presume was too weighty for the smaller. However, it is evident that keeping up steam and therefore motion for ten minutes would have won the Crystal Palace prize of £50 and separately the Society's prize would be advantageously competed for £95 — viz the lightest engine in proportion to its power. These are two elements which are quite irrespective of size — weight and power — and they should be readily determined. I should therefore decidedly exhibit it.

'Spencer the flying man provides himself with a plane which extends over his back and continues tail-like some 14 feet behind him. He runs, then hitches feet up, and works a short pair of wings with arms, but am doubtful whether he will have all ready in time for the Exhibition as he keeps improving his apparatus and succeeding better (so he says) each time.

'As you are aware, the Society is badly off for funds, but when you are assured of success, let me know what you will want for the purpose of exhibiting.'

*　　　*　　　*

There was now only a month to go before the Exhibition opened. Stringfellow's small triplane was ready and the engine tested, but there had been no opportunity of trying it in flight. However, he had designed a simulated launching suspension so that the machine could run in captive flight below a wire spanning on high the width of the Crystal Palace. Free flight was not permitted because of the risk of fire. On 4 June Stringfellow wrote to Brearey: 'It would be desirable to know positively if the model could be exhibited in the interior. I should wish to know the length and height of the building clear of everything. I shall make it go from one end to the other BY SOME MEANS. My model was made for indoor experiment. Perhaps it might be tried outdoors on a fine day. I think I have told you all through that my difficulty has been want of room for experimental testing. Necessity has driven me into some experiments in this direction which appear to point out the probability of utilising the invention in rather a novel and useful manner. Should this be the case the application I think ought to have protection. What do you think? The machinery and things generally work very well, but I am not certain the sustaining planes use the best possible arrangement. The model works about ten minutes and at thirty miles per hour, so you see it must travel some distance.

'I don't know what Spencer is doing, but should suppose he is working in the right direction, and I should think his experiments would have a tendency to popularise the true principles of flight.'

Brearey's reply is missing, but the Aeronautical Society's Secretary was not a technical man and apparently had misunderstood, for on 10 June Stringfellow wrote: 'I am sorry if I have said anything to mislead you. In the letter you referred to I stated I would make it go from one end to the other of the building BY SOME MEANS. This can be done by a guideline and certainly in the first experiments I should not attempt to liberate it till it had thoroughly proved capable of self-control. Whatever shortcoming there may be at first, there is nothing in the principle that may not eventually be surmounted. I wish that Mr Wenham could have seen the model. He would have understood at once.

'There is no room sufficiently large for experimenting in this neighbourhood or I should not have kept my old models rotting for years.'

A day or two later he received a letter from Brearey written on 9 June: 'I have accepted hitherto what you have said as facts, believing you to be cautious and since your last letter I had spoken of your machinery going from end to end of the building and possibly being able to go three miles in ten minutes. I have a meeting of the Exhibition Committee tomorrow, when possibly I

The turnpike cottage on Snowdon Hill. Turn left to Bala Down.

Stringfellow's actual successful 1848 model photographed in his studio.

A Science Museum reproduction of the 1847-8 model showing the method of launching in a carriage suspended from a wire.

The smithy and adjacent Independent chapel in Fore Street.

Stringfellow's 'Bat' model with a background showing the wings of other models and propellers of various sizes. Also visible are a crashed wing and a small cabin on the left and a propeller frame and engine in the foreground.

John Stringfellow in his late fifties.

The first Aeronautical Exhibition,
Crystal Palace 1868, showing the Stringfellow
triplane model and the cabin of
Ariel on the right.

Frederick Brearey, Secretary of the
Aeronautical Society, 1866-96.

The Science Museum replica of the 1868 triplane, which differs considerably from the model in the Smithsonian which was reconstructed from the components supplied by Frederick John Stringfellow.

The engine and boiler from the triplane of 1868.

William Samuel Henson, aged fifty-four.

Stringfellow's armoured hand cart behind which two gunmen could crouch and fire through apertures.

A two cylinder steam engine for the French airship.

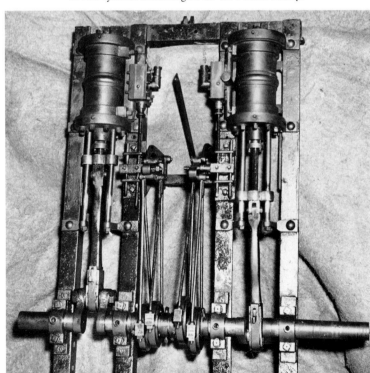

may be authorised to run down to Chard on Saturday by first train if I find one to suit me — but meanwhile can you make an arrangement to send the Model to a more suitable place where experiments can be made? I will engage to pay the expense of hiring premises until the time arrives for the Exhibition.'

The following day a second letter confirmed he would be in Chard on Saturday afternoon by Express train starting at 10.15 and arriving at 3.20 pm. 'Please engage a bed for one at an Inn.'

Tantalisingly there is no record of what happened on this historic occasion but trials of the tri-plane under power must certainly have been made at about that time to ensure flying trim, for Stringfellow and his dentist son next took a train to London and managed to assemble the machine and complete the difficult task of rigging the 'flight guideline' cable in time for the ceremonial opening of the Exhibition on 25 June, where there were seventy-seven exhibits. These included kites, model airships and model heavier-than-air machines — with Stringfellow's impressive twin-propeller triplane high overhead. Of the heavier-than-air machines, two were helicopters, two had fixed wings, and the rest had flapping wings. Fifteen engines, including Stringfellow's, were submitted for the £100 reward offered by the Society for the lightest power/weight ratio — eight steam, five gas or oil, and two employing gun-cotton. Only Stringfellow's two steam engines, and a miniature by the Frenchman Camille Vert which was too small to measure its power, were demonstrated in motion.

The Exhibition attracted great numbers of spectators, most of whom gazed in bewilderment at the inventive projects which were alleged to open the new age of aerial navigation. Twice a day steam was got up in the triplane and runs made along the wire. This tended to become a social occasion, and the bearded 27 year-old Edward, Prince of Wales, was a particularly interested spectator.

The Morning Star reported: 'The model was attached by means of a travelling pulley to a horizontal line which became raised several feet, thus showing the tendency of the machine to rise in the air.' The rival *Standard* stated more emphatically: 'In the course of its flight the Aerial Carriage had an evident tendency to rise in the air, as was seen by the fact that the line on which it was suspended, and along which the pulley travelled, was raised several feet.'

An interesting letter to Mrs John Stringfellow from her niece Rose gives the atmosphere of the crowded Exhibition: 'I should have written you before but we have been so busy that I have not been able to get out in time to go to the Palace to see Uncle's Model before opening day. However I went in last night, but not till late. It was a grand day for Uncle. The Prince and Princess of Wales and Prince Alfred and several of the Princesses with their train of attendants were there. The Prince was so charmed with the Model that he sent the Duke of Sutherland to ask Uncle to go to the Royal Box.

'Mr and Mrs Smith were there and had a long chat with Fred. They came back yesterday and told me of Uncle's success, so tomorrow I hope to see the little affair fly across the nave. I am going in the afternoon. I called to see the Smiths this morning before I came to Julia's as I was in hope they would have spent the day here with us, but they had so many engagements.

'Of course Uncle has won the prize. How I wish you could have come with them; it would have been such a nice treat for you. I hope you have someone with you while Uncle is away. How is Laura? Give her my love. Your affectionate niece, Rose.'

During the course of the eleven-day exhibition members of the Aeronautical Society gathered for three official meetings, at the second of which, on 1 July, Stringfellow was present and Wenham declared to his fellow members that Stringfellow's triplane was made on a perfectly correct principle, whereupon the latter was pressed for more details of his successful trials of 20 years previously. However, the account purporting to be what he said, as printed in the Society's annual Report at the end of 1868, is probably garbled, for in those days there were no stenographers, so an attempt had to be made by the Secretary writing long-hand but unable to keep pace with the speaker. Those who have had that experience know how imperfect the consequent Minutes of a meeting can be. The pioneer's reported reply is therefore a *précis* in the form:

> 'Mr Stringfellow: in reply to a question said the length of his plane is 21 ft frontage, with 28 ft of sustaining surface. The plane could be extended to a larger subject with great facility.'

There he was referring to the triplane 'frontage' as the sum of the spans, whereas his other bigger models were monoplanes of half that amount. At this point either he became confused or a question was interjected about the original great 20 ft model which he and Henson had tested, for the Report continues, 'In making and trying his machine by day he had been so annoyed by followers, that he resolved to make experiments at night. They were favoured by beautiful moonlight, but after being out about ten minutes there was a relaxation in the wings of the machine which he did not understand. He found they were drenched with dew, and nothing could be done.' The next sentence switches back to the triplane: 'He had tried a great many experiments and had come to the conclusion that the minimum speed of his little model would be 20 miles an hour.'

The Report continued verbatim: 'Mr Brearey: It really did fly?' — but now is referring to the epoch making model that made the world's first power flight. 'Mr Stringfellow: It really did fly in 1847.'

On 3 July at the third meeting he was reported to have said he would like to make a few remarks with reference to the triplane, but again his comments are bowdlerized: 'It was not intended for outdoor or rough work. It had sustaining planes, urged forward by propellers at a given angle, at an inclination of about 1 in 60. He had run it along a wire and after going a little distance had thrown it off. He had driven the model along a room a number of times, and that was how he wished to try this model. It was not constructed to go out, but he was ready to make the attempt. He would throw it off, and if it must fail it must fail. He disliked Exhibitions.'

In terms of the Report, the Chairman quizzed him further:

Do we understand you are prepared to exhibit your model set free in the open air?

Mr Stringfellow: I will throw the model off, and it it does not fly it will break its neck. If it gets ahead out of doors it will fly for some time.

The Chairman: I am sure all the members of the Society will be very much pleased if you will make the experiments.

Mr Stringfellow: The model will be ready sometime after the next few days.

The Chairman: They had the advantage of some description of Mr Stringfellow's machine, which, in his opinion, was the most practical they had had before them yet, so far as the Exhibition was concerned; and he thought if they had only succeeded in bringing that one machine there, they ought to say it had been a great success.

No contemporary report of a free flight attempt has been found, but fifteen years later Brearey wrote: 'In the basement afterwards, the author assisted to hold a canvas with which to break the fall of the model when liberated. When freed, it descended an incline with apparent lightness until it caught in the canvas; but the impression conveyed to us was that had there been sufficient fall it would have recovered itself. It was intended at the last to set the model free in the open country, but it was found that the engine, which had done much work, required repairs. Many months afterwards, in the presence of the author, an experiment was tried in a field at Chard by means of a wire stretched across it. The engine was fed with methylated spirits, and during some portion of its run under the wire the draft occasioned thereby invariably extinguished the flames and so these interesting trials were rendered abortive.'

*   *   *

The Exhibition having run its course with great success, Frederick Brearey notified John Stringfellow on 21 July: 'It affords me great pleasure to be able to confirm my opinion and wishes by announcing to you the award of the £100 prize. I have done this in an official letter. I will add to this if you like, the weight of water and fuel, and then you might like to get the letter put in print.

'I now enclose cheque for £25 more. We are making an effort to abstain from calling upon the guarantors and this can only be done be waiting for the payment of subscriptions as they fall due. I believe also that we shall secure something from the Crystal Palace. Don't however hesitate to let me know (as a friend) when the next remittance would be acceptable.'

Apparently his daughter was staying with the Stringfellows, for he continues: 'Now about my little girl. I am much afraid she will become a nuisance. An only child is generally an unbearable child, and I am afraid she is no exception. There is some chance of my wife and me coming to Seaton (don't say a word to Lily) next Saturday, for I see there is an excursion train and in that case it will be as cheap as any place. The only thing is as to lodging, for I suppose we shall crawl along and get there late, but all this I have to enquire about. If you think we could get everything clean and humble for 14/- or 15/- per week, that would suit us very well for say a fortnight, and we could take our little girl away either next Saturday or the Saturday after so that at least she could have a week at the seaside. With kind regards to Mrs Stringfellow.'

Hitherto letters had been formally addressed, 'Dear Sir', but henceforth it was 'My dear Sir' and 'I remain, my dear Sir, yours very Truly'.

Enclosed with the personal letter was the official announcement: 'At a Council meeting held yesterday at the Duke of Sutherland's, you were awarded the prize of £100 for light engines. Data for estimating the power was area of piston 3 ins; pressure in cylinders 80 lbs per square inch; length of stroke 3 ins; velocity of piston 150 ft per minute; so 3 x 80 x 150 = 36,000 foot pounds; this makes rather more than one horse power. The weight of the engine and boiler is only 13 pounds and is probably the lightest steam engine ever constructed. The engine, boiler, car and propellers together were afterwards weighed, but without water and fuel, and found to be 16 pounds.'

So impressed with the engine were visiting engineering enthusiasts that they had contributed a further £50, and with the combined money Stringfellow built a long room at Chard for flight experiments almost certainly made in conjunction with his son Frederick John who had assisted him throughout the Exhibition. However there was no prize for the model triplane, but the Jurors' Committee Report specifically stated: 'It was seen by several that after a certain velocity had been attained, the machine left the support of the wire and rose up. On one occasion the wire broke just after the start, but the buoyant power of the planes caused so light a descent that no damage occurred. The model was remarkable for the elegance and neatness of its construction, and was the first experiment adopting the proposed system of superposed aeroplanes to a steam flying machine. Mr Stringfellow will, no doubt, ascertain the value of these by comparative experiments, with which he is now occupied.'

On 25 August he received a more personal letter from Brearey: 'Much has happened to unsettle me since I last wrote to you, and much remains for disquietude since my father-in-law's death. A full year must elapse before things can be settled and property here and in the West Indies can be sold.

'Mr R Merryweather of Clapham House has authorised to pay his prize of £22 to you and I now enclose a cheque for £27.2s — which will leave £25 due to you. Perhaps you would like to write and thank him. He has not had the Report yet, which I now send you, but I wrote of your engine and asked him how I was to dispose of his prize. You should soon become a Member of our Society.

'I am suffering from Lumbago and can hardly sit up, but I will send you some more Reports when I get the bulk. We often talk of you all and wonder how you are getting on with Laura. My wife joins in very kind regards to you and Mrs Stringfellow. Lily sends kisses to you all.'

Laura was the Stringfellows' 20 year-old invalid daughter probably suffering from undiagnosed consumption and of great concern to her parents. Meanwhile Brearey wrote on 6 September: 'Application has been made to me to write an account for a popular periodical of the more promising novelties exhibited at the Crystal Palace — to be accompanied with illustrations. Foremost is your Aerial Machine. Would you mind setting down and writing for me a short history of your common concern with Henson? How you worked out your ideas — the trials and supposed cause of failure — your next attempt and trials at Cremorne; results, causes of your abandoning that form and taking to superposed planes; your reasons for not setting it free at the Crystal Palace. I have ½ photograph of which they must make a woodcut.

'If you had time (to give details) I should like to describe your engine — with photographs of engine and boiler — commencing with your former attempts to secure lightness. Don't be particular about the style. I only want the matter and will put it into shape if you will kindly give the statement in the order in which I have written it. They want it about the 10th but I am afraid you cannot do it by that time so I want to make it interesting if not amusing.'

Stringfellow's reply certainly took some time, but on 21 September he wrote: 'I have sent off photos of the little machine with which I had the partial success in 1847 and '48. No 1 gives you a direct view of the upper surface of wing and tail, the length of each wing is 5 ft and 2 ft in the widest part, both containing about thirteen feet of sustaining surface, and the tail a little over 2 ft. I left the cabin open at the top that you may see how the machinery is arranged. By a magnifier you will see the propellers are much broken but I think there is sufficient left to enable you to see their construction, but this you will see best by referring to No 4. The blades are very wide, occupying ¾ of the circumference. Each blade is 8 inches long and set at a pitch of about 60°. The reason I made them so wide was at the time I had the impression, whether right or wrong, that a wider blade would be required in a medium as yielding as air to get the desired effect. I always considered that I sacrificed some power by clothing the blades down to the shaft. Still I do not think the effect produced has been much if any exceeded in my later efforts. When I got the thing up to a flying speed, the machine slanted up in a similar manner to a pheasant, but this is a question I must now try to set at rest by making an arrangement that will record and measure the effects produced by different width blades at different angles in relation to the power of the engine. Should you require more photos, please let me know, and any information I can supply shall be happy to do so.'

Then he adds a most significant statement that 'I am engaged in experimenting with a view of ultimately constructing a larger machine that would be sufficient to carry a person to guide and conduct it.'

His letter continues: 'Henson and me generally took the rook as our standard as carrying ½ lb to a foot. This bird can be seen any day leisurely flying at a speed not more than 20 miles an hour and we considered that if we kept our machine within these limits we had a fair chance of success. I am apprehensive we shall find our shortcoming not because we have too much or too little sustaining surface as there must be a wide margin, but the real difficulty is to make the full power of the engine available. This I do not think we have ever done with the present arrangements and proportion of our propellers.

'Henson did full as much as could be expected with the means he had and in the infant state of the science. He made a spring model which illustrated the principal and several hand launched models, and if his experiments at the Adelaide Gallery were abortive, they were not fruitless. The thing might have been different had the parties spent less money in rousing the public's expectation and more enabling Mr Henson to carry on the experiments and mature his plans. Henson is a friend of mine and of course I knew something of the treatment he received from the parties he was connected with.

'The Batwing Model of which I first sent you a photo you do not name. This I consider a more perfect Model than the one I had at Cremorne, but I was not able to try it (fully) for want of a room. In my opinion it would have made the best plate.

'I believe the engine in the Crystal Palace Model, according to calculations made there by some of the engineers who examined it, was more than one third of an horse power. You have the dimensions in my former paper to you. I have several photos of the steam engine, but have not a very good one. Will send one of the best.'

Brearey's acknowledgement of Stringfellow's letter raised the crucial question of stability: 'I have received the photos alright. I shall adopt one of them for a woodcut. I presume this is the one which flew at Cremorne? I am now embodying the substance of your remarks and I must note as I go on those things which require a little clearing up, for what strikes me may strike others.

'You speak of the trial by night as abortive because of the drooping of the wings. One is induced naturally to enquire why the experiments were not continued in the day time where the wings had become rigid again?

'Wise, in speaking of this attempt says: "To the practical man it at once occurs what is to keep it from tilting over and losing its balance by a flaw of wind, or any other casualty, and then tumbling to the ground, admitting that it could raise itself up and move forward?" The same I think could be said of yachts or any other craft carrying a large surface of sail. In these, the keel plays an important part, and I fancy that in aerial machines it must occupy a still more prominent place.

'You give the weight of the entire machine as from 25 to 28 lbs. Did that include the Engine, or what was the proportion of weight to surface? If it included the Engine the surface seems superabundant and more than the stated calculations of the full-size machine would require, viz 1 sq ft for each ½ lb. This is all that strikes me just now.'

The quoted comment was pertinent, and taken from John Wise's book *A System of Aeronautics* published in 1850. Without fin or dihedral, Stringfellow models had adequate longitudinal stability, but if side-slip ensued, the underhung cabin would increase the lateral inclination and cause the machine to make an ever increasing curving descent. However, his basic intention was limited to the prime object of 'making a steam engine fly', and from practical experience he knew that in calm air a finless winged machine, on the analogy of a bird, could fly directionally straight for a while, and that was all he wanted.

Brearey's next letter, on 26 September, did not pursue this matter of stability but informed him that: 'Major John Scott Phillips whose Paper appears in one of the Annual Reports, and who seems to have for many years paid great attention to Aerial locomotion, has designed a plan for a light steam motor power and I met him by appointment the other day to receive explanation. Wenham has seen the plans and says he should like to see them tried. I told Phillips of yours and that you were also making steam Engines and that I would, if he liked, send the plans for your inspection, at which he seemed pleased.

'Thanks for your letter. Did I not make some remarks about the difference in the sustaining surface in proportion to weight of the Crystal Palace model and the successful flying one?'

Three days later Stringfellow wrote saying: 'I received the drawings for which I thank you. Major Phillips's paper in the Annual Report, and the observations of the flight of Vultures in India proves in my opinion that he is no casual observer and anything emanating from him is worthy of attention.

'I consider his plans very novel and ingenious and should much like to see them tried although I must say I do not see so clear the mode of operation as the inventor, but I trust he will be borne out in his view as to simplicity and lightness for an engine of given power. I will return the papers in a day or two. I want to devote a little more time to them.

'I believe I gave you the respective weight and surface of each Model, and by comparing you will see the difference of sustaining surface in proportion to weight. The Cremorne model at 17 square feet of sustaining surface, 6 lb weight, giving little less than 6 ounces to a foot. Crystal Palace model 13 square feet sustaining surface, 12 lbs weight which is also near six ounces to a foot. I was not aware the two models carried so near. I added surface after without advantage as you recollect.'

Crossing that letter was one from Brearey enclosing 'four notes and a P.O. £3.19s, having deducted from the remainder of the prize money (£25) £1.15s. for your Subscription.'

Intent as always in notifying Stringfellow of rival experimenters or possible purchasers of a steam engine, Brearey wrote on 5 November: 'Mr De Perring called on me and said that he had come from Calcutta purposely to lay before our Society his plans, but he did not enter into them then — he was to write particulars. We naturally talked about your ideas. He seemed struck with the light motive power and I expect he wants to see you about this. I know nothing of him and you must judge how far it will be advisable to let him into your designs.

'Our correspondent, Mr Jas. W. Ward of West 47 St New York, says: "If Mr Stringfellow could furnish drawings of his Engine I will have an illustrated account of it published in a suitable journal in this City, but perhaps he would not care to do this until he has secured his rights therein."

'The Bat's wing model which you spoke of, I could not find space for, as I thought it best to give the illustration of what was demonstrated as successful.'

On 23 December Brearey notified Stringfellow that: 'The Council is determined upon not having another Exhibition without first hearing what objects are likely to be sent. Please say if you intend to exhibit and what. I am sending out this circular.

'I hope to hear that your health is at any rate not worse than when I last saw you. We all join in sincere wishes for such happiness as falls to the lot of the happiest at this Season, especially to you and all yours.'

Chapter 9
A Valued Friendship

By 1869, England's trade and finance were beginning to show signs of substantial recovery from the collapse of 1866, and everyone seemed confident that Mr Gladstone as Premier would deal adequately with the great questions of the day. Even France remained at peace with her neighbours, and in America old wounds were being overlooked and General Grant had been inaugurated President. There was news also that Frederick Marriott, as a citizen of San Francisco, was attempting to patent a dirigible which had lifting wings, described as an 'Aerial Steam Car' which he named *Avitor* — reflecting the long gone associations with Henson and Stringfellow's Aerial Steam Carriage *Ariel*.

Despite ill health, John Stringfellow's interests remained as wide as ever. As a sideline it seems he was making calliper joints for an artificial limb business set up at Chard by the local high class shoe maker, John Gillingham. The two men became close friends, and in later years Gillingham did considerable propaganda work in commemorating the prowess of Stringfellow.

Brearey's article on 'Flying Machines' was published in the January *Popular Science* but though he stated that 'Mr Stringfellow is now engaged in experimenting with a view of ultimately constructing a large machine that would be sufficient to carry a person to guide and conduct it, and on this scale he will avoid many difficulties which are inseparable from small models,' it was not until after receipt of his prize money that the old man was able to build a shed over 70 feet long to accommodate it. Family tradition has it that with his son Frederick John to help, flight trials of models were eventually made in that shed though the immediate task was construction of more small steam engines, as well as operating their respective professions. Thus in January 1869 Stringfellow was advertising that 'Portraits can be taken in every style of art from the smallest miniature to lifesize'. His seventh son, Edward, and Fred's eldest son, Frederick William Henson Stringfellow, had also trained as photographers and established themselves in Eddy, Mexico, but initially travelled as far as Peru, where in 1866 they had taken the only surviving photograph of the then 54 year-old side-whiskered and moustached William Samuel Henson, Frederick's namesake. Though long out of touch, Stringfellow retained high regard for his early partner who had so ambitiously promoted the design of the epoch-making 'Aerial Carriage'.

Paul Johnston, when Director of the USA's Smithsonian Aeronautical Museum in 1943, reported that: 'From 1867 Henson listed no business connection. He considered himself a consulting engineer, an enterprise that was not always profitable. There were times when his family was said to have been in somewhat straightened circumstances. At one period, probably from the spring of 1864 to late in 1866, he lived in Lima, Peru. Why he was there or what he was doing is not accurately known. Letters and other family records indicate that he had some work there with an engineering project, probably connected with the construction of a bridge or with a mining venture. In January 1869, a United States' patent covering a centrifugal screw pump was issued jointly to Henson and to a John White of Lima.'

In similar manner to John Stringfellow's wide interest in everything from botany and ornithology to steam engines and electricity: 'Henson was continually thinking up new ideas in mechanics and machinery, and he would work intensely on such things for a time, then drop it — a new razor, a breach loading cannon, a method of water-proofing fabrics, an ice-machine, or a device for cleaning cisterns. Latterly he became increasingly interested in the mechanics of the universe, and in the spring of 1871 published a privately printed treatise entitled *The Great Facts of Modern Astronomy*, with an exposition of what they teach, comprising the formation of the sun and stars, the cause of rotary motion, the formation of planets and their satellites, solution of the law of distances, theory of light, and the sun spots.'

However, he more modestly concluded his book by saying: 'I make no pretentions to be an astronomer, or to enter into the extreme exactness of that exalted science, but the business of my life has made me familiar with mechanical motions: and believing that I had traced the motions of the planets to their source, I have undertaken in my own way, to make it known. If it is truth, as I believe it to be, it will stand, and if it can be shown that it is not true, let it fall.'

Though Stringfellow's philosophy was not so abstruse, a letter from Brearey on 22 April 1869 reveals that currently he had been pursuing his inventive way with an armoured hand-cart which enabled the crew to maintain continual gunfire while moving forward towards the enemy front, or even to retire without danger! Here Brearey deals with the possibility of patenting it, as well as revealing the happy social relationship with Stringfellow: 'Your letter greatly tempts me to pay you a visit. It smacks of business and pleasure combined — a happy conjunction for the conscience. You have spoken to me before about the invention for war purposes, but I did not encourage it, fearing that through it, you might neglect the other; but you speak also of experimenting upon the Crystal Palace model first. Now it is possible that if I were invited to witness these experiments I might be able to charge my fare there and back to the Society, and would then enter into the other matter.

'Unless you have committed your ideas to others and have cause to be afraid, I would not hurry to patent, for it not only marks with certainty a period which must end with greater outlay, or else the entire abandonment of a conviction which is no longer a secret. I believe that an intention kept secret would be more valuable to a government than a parchment patent which is no secret. Of course these observations must be modified according to the nature of the invention, but doubtless I could be of service in its proper introduction, having the entrée to several influential quarters.

'I must however get my General Meeting of Members over before I can leave here. I am waiting in the house now for the Annual Report which you will have in a post or two. After they are posted I shall call a Council and arrange at the Society of Arts for a meeting, so I might perhaps be able to visit you about 15th or 20th of May, but I am sorry to say without wife or child. I profess a conscience, but nevertheless my wife sends her kind love to yours and says she hopes to see her before Christmas comes. As for myself I look forward with renewed youth to our rambles, and to a little bit of trout fishing in the best month of the year.'

There is no account of that happy visit, but Stringfellow decided to go ahead with a patent for an 'Improved apparatus for affording protection from bullets and other missiles', and in July he filed a Provisional Specification and drawings.

Meantime he wrote to Brearey on 9 July: 'Have you any thought of attending the Scientific Meeting at Exeter? I should think you might read a Paper on the principles of flight. I could make a nice hand-model to be thrown to illustrate the principle or I could take the Crystal Palace model there if they would find me a room 100 feet long. I believe I have it in better condition than ever it has been before. I am putting on the superposed planes and doing what I can to make the thing complete for a trial. It would keep the thing alive, which ought to be an advantage to the Society. Drop me a line and tell me what you think of it.

'Kind regards to Mrs Brearey and dear Lily, trusting you are all well.'

Here again is proof of Stringfellow's continuing aeronautical experimenting with models; but *inter alia* he was not only greatly admired by Brearey but also inspired him in his work for the Aeronautical Society.

On the 13th of July Brearey wrote: 'I hardly know what to say about your proposition to read a Paper at Exeter; however not to lose time and by way of paving the approaches, I have written to B. S. Ellis at Exeter, one of the local Secretaries, who I believe is the Mayor, to ask if there be 100 ft accommodation in the room provided for the mechanical section. The next is what can I say of sufficient interest? Can you give me some ideas?' This certainly indicates that he regarded John Stringfellow as an authority, and echoes the similar relationship with Henson in earlier years.

The Mayor, writing from the Albert Memorial Museum, promptly replied to Brearey but forgot to put in the figure for length, 'The room in which Section B meets is only (blank) feet, but there is a large gravelled playground outside where a line could be easily suspended if you think the room not large enough for your purposes. The Victoria Hall, where the evening lecture and address will be delivered is 129 feet in length, and you could doubtless have that to exhibit the Aerial Machine, which I think would be an attraction to many of the Members and Associates.'

Brearey enclosed this letter with one of his on 15th July saying: 'I am short of paper and am anxious to get this off today. I send you the Mayor of Exeter's reply and mine to him. Send me your opinion.

'I would like what I have to say made interesting on the spot. Can you either by spring power cause your walking stick model to continue its flight, or can you attach a small spring to the paper dart perhaps made a little stiffer, or give me the walking stick without the spring and the paper one with it so as to take it along the room? We shall then come off with *flying* colours.

'Has the patent been granted yet?'

His reference to a spring refers to lengths of twisted elastic in tension which Stringfellow may have devised, though ascribed as an invention of the Frenchman Pénaud in the following year. Stringfellow mentions these 'rubber bands' in his letter of the same date as Brearey's whom he tells: 'I have sent you a fresh list of Patents which I received yesterday. The changes appear to be truly and clearly stated.

'With regard to the Meeting at Exeter you say you have written to enquire if they have 100 ft accommodation in the mechanical section. Now 100 feet would scarcely be enough for anything as I don't think less than 50 feet run would be sufficient to start the Machine before it was released from the wire, yet is the experiment to be abandoned for want of the impulsive force which the Frenchman gives his Bat in throwing off? I am doing everything I can towards construction of models but it consumes a great deal of time. However, I shall do the best I can and let you know as early as possible. I can't get any india rubber bands of any length in Chard for this purpose.'

That letter reached Brearey next day and he immediately replied: 'You have bothered me about the room, but I send you back your letter to show you that the mistake did not originate with me. Here it is — "100 feet long" plain enough. Now I did not know that you contemplated setting it free or I should have gauged it myself that 100 feet would not be long enough. I wish you could go to Exeter and call upon the Mayor and see the place for yourself. There are cheap fares now and I contemplate paying you a visit before I go to Exeter, but of course if we cannot secure a proper place we must abandon the idea altogether.

'Please send me back your letter as I have occasion to show it. Mr Glaisher thinks I ought to go. Of course much depends upon whether I can get up a sufficiently interesting Paper, but I calculated much upon what might be enabled to show in the way of models. I should begin by simply throwing off a lot of those paper ones. I would then start off your stick, and if possible I should like to prolong the flight of the small one by means of a spring working screw blades, and finish up all by your Aerial Machine. I do believe then that we might not only secure a hearty reception, but through the prominence given in every newspaper to the British Association the experiments would attract that notice which it so much requires.'

There must have been further letters from Stringfellow, for on 24 July Brearey wrote: 'Your letter of this morning discourages me and renders my reading of a Paper doubtful. I must now disclose my little game. I don't want to read a Paper which will provoke any discussion and consequently require me to answer. Now I thought that at the close of my Paper I could announce to the audience that by adjourning to the playground they could witness your Machine and I could at once divert their attention and under cover of it, slip away. I do not feel myself sufficiently a champion of Aerial Navigation to defend all I may write but I want to make what I *do* say interesting so as to gain support for the Society. This I can do by some trifling experiments. I might for instance show a form of Aerial Machine and its flight from my hand — viz the paper dart and your stick. I might show another form of plane — viz the principle of the Frenchman's Bat which might glide from a gallery if there be one. By easy graduation I might show how flight could be continued if you could help me with the dart or other spring arrangement to a different fall, and to crown all might invite the audience to witness a system of superposed planes capable of carrying its own steam Engine and boiler by simply moving out of doors into the playground. Now I send you a plan of the ground where apparently you may get a run of 271 feet, and it is this that I had hoped you would see at Exeter. Have you got one of the Frenchman's Bats? If not I will send you one. We ought to get one up on a larger scale.

'The title of my paper ought to be "*Mechanical Flight* by Mr F. W. Brearey illustrated by Mr Stringfellow". I feel certain that if we can manage this programme with any additions suggested by yourself, we shall attract universal attention. If the playground is impracticable I must give up my Paper, but that need not hinder you from exhibiting at the Victorial Hall.'

That was followed two days later by another letter. He was nervously depending on Stringfellow as the authority: 'I think I have made a mistake. I fancied that the Victoria Hall is the one where the people assembled in the Evening. Of course this is the Hall devoted to the mechanical section. It will be better than any playground. So get everything ready so that you could be independent of me in case difficulties arise which I cannot surmount, and which alone might prevent me going to Exeter. Can you manage a spring, either for your stick model or the dart shape? Our Chairman stated the other evening that he had one some years ago which flew very well as long as the spring power lasted. I should say your stick would form a capital framework to stretch a piece of guttapersha along its length and turn a screw.

'Can you think of any simple arrangement whereby I can liberate the Bat which should hang head down from the ceiling and fall if we touch a silk thread? I think if you will try this from the roof of your workshop that it will recover itself and fly right onwards. My rooms are not high enough. Don't forget to tell me if it will do so and whether it is possible to liberate it from the ceiling. I have three, so I send you one as you did not say that you had one. As I am writing my Paper and am working up to my demonstrations, please let me know what I can depend upon. There's nothing like experiments if they are ever so simple for reaching interest.

'I shall go to town today to see about the Patent so shall take this letter with me and post from thence. Brooman says he has had certain queries addressed to him by the Attorney-General which he has answered and cannot understand the reasons of the delay as other patents have been granted since. He has just sent up to the office while I wait. No-one is in (the Patent Office). They will send a reply.

'I send the Bat inside the *Mechanics Magazine* in which there is a report of our meeting.'

Meanwhile Stringfellow had visited Exeter to examine the premises, leading to his reply on 19 July: 'I received the Magazine with the *News Letter* for which I am much obliged. I don't feel exactly clear about the arrangements at Exeter. I spent so much time in looking for the Mayor that I had little left for anything else. I suppose I must run down again.

'It is my old friend Marriott (mentioned in the News Letter) that is getting all the sensation in San Francisco with the flying balloon — the same person who got up the excitement here when Henson took out the patent in connection with Colombine, and I trust you will succeed in raising some tin by it as it may be to my advantage as he owes me £100 with interest. I think if he had the means he would pay it.

'That line in my letter said 100 *yards*, but this supposed we should not be likely to get it. I am trying experiments at my rooms to ascertain the distance for starting and I find after it has gone about 60 feet it has accumulated a tremendous force far greater than I ever had before. I wish my room had been double the size. I could then settle the question. It must be settled indoors before anything can be done out.'

But this letter left crucial points unexplained, and on 5 August Brearey wrote to him: 'I am obliged to bother you with my remarks as time is short. In the first place did the India-rubber do? Or shall I send you some more? Spencer showed me how it should be tied, viz, while on full stretch. He also advised that when that was done, to fly it in a grass field where its fall would not injure it as his was broken to pieces with knocks. This will answer your question.

'Shall I tell you what in my own uneducated mind I imagined I would make in thinking of a spring? I beg you not to laugh, but attribute my idea to ignorance. I would have made a drum wheel, round which I would have wound India-rubber at its greatest tension. My drum wheel should be capable of being regulated to offer more or less resistence by means of a screw. When wound up at greatest tension I would attach the end to a multiplying gear connected with the screw blades, which the stretched India-rubber would revolve regularly because of the friction of the drum wheel.

By these means I thought the power of the spring might be made to last some time. Otherwise it would go off in a whirl — you see what a fool I am!

'I am exceedingly glad to hear you say that the Bat can be thrown from the ceiling. The next thing is, will they allow it to be done? I am the more pleased as I have written my Paper so far as the Bat illustration. I wish I had a larger model on this principle.

'It occurred to me if this Paper and its accompanying experiments were successful, I might lay myself open to deliver lectures throughout the country, sharing the proceeds with you or your son Fred in return for managing the Aerial Machine. No doubt I shall have to engage recruits, and it will doubtless increase the number of our members. I promise that my Paper shall be interesting but I confess I look to your success in the spring model for much of the éclat attaching to it.'

Brearey then diverts to talk of Stringfellow's patent for the armoured vehicle saying: 'It looks exceedingly strange about the Patent. In one sense it looks favourable. Can it be possible that as Lord Grosvenor said he should recommend it to Mr Caldwell, the matter has come before him and it is being considered by the Minister of War? I shall go and see about it.'

He continues: 'My soul longs to be with you, but my body is the incubus which cannot be conveyed upon the instant. It is something however to be able to sit at one's table and be able to communicate one's ideas.'

There the correspondence ends for the time being. What eventually happened about the lecture and demonstration has not been documented, but there certainly was an Exeter meeting of the British Association for the Advancement of Science in the latter part of August, though no mention can be found of any talks or demonstrations by Brearey and Stringfellow. Maybe there are reports in local newspaper archives but it has not been possible to investigate in detail. Nevertheless these letters again re-affirm that at almost 70, Stringfellow was still actively engaged in aeronautical experiments with models.

*   *   *

The complete Armoured Vehicle Specification, with modified drawings, was accepted on 1 January 1870, and defined a flat steel plate some five feet in length, mounted on two carriage wheels like a hand cart but tiltable to about 45 degrees so that two gunmen could crouch behind with gun muzzles protruding through apertures at a convenient height. Ammunition and breech loaders or other arms could be stored in the body of the vehicle, or a small field gun carried in a heavier model. The top of the cartridge box could be extended to shield the handle frame, and a small front support wheel prevented the main shield embedding in the ground. Stringfellow proposed that it could be used as a single fighting unit or a number of vehicles be arranged side by side to form a small moveable fortress or in a square with canvas roof as a largely bullet-proof tent. However there is no record of the army purchasing these machines, though this apparatus was the precursor of armoured artillery and the tank.

He had hoped to sell these machines to France, for there had been antagonism between that country and Prussia since the defeat of Austria in 1866, and on 19 July 1870 war broke out between the two. Germany joined Prussia to form a well-prepared army, yet the French commanded by Marshal Bazaine seemed in confusion, and it was not until ten days later that the Emperor Napoleon III assumed military command. In the ensuing weeks France suffered defeat after defeat and on 4 September Napoleon was deposed by his people. In Paris a Republic was proclaimed from the Hotel de Ville, and the city began an heroic resistance, defended by its heavily armed outer rim of forts, though that was no barricade to the shells from the up-dated German artillery. Communication to the outside world became a problem. However it was known that balloons had been used for air observation in the American Civil War, so they were now employed to great effect from the beleaguered city, and in the course of four months sixty-five floated away in succession carrying a total of 12 metric tonnes of mail, 164 people and six dogs, as well as 370 pigeons with the novel aim of using their winged return to bring back messages photographed in miniature. Stringfellow had contacts with the Parisians because of earlier exports of his small engines, and had constructed a steam engine to power a small French dirigible. More than 20 years later his son Frederick John described this power plant as a much larger engine with two cylinders 2½ or 3 inch diameter, with copper boiler cones. 'It was begun by my father for a company for the relief of Paris by Balloon, but the siege was raised before it was completed.'

Though no correspondence has been located between Brearey and Stringfellow from the early days of the Franco-Prussian war to the new year, the general tenor must have been maintained, for on 31 January 1870 Brearey wrote to his old friend: 'Passing over all that is provoking in the information you give me in your letter (with regard to the Patent), I went to see Brooman today. He does not think things are as bad as Payne reports. Certainly the superiority in your Patent is very conspicuous, for I have seen the drawings of both — viz yours in the *Mechanics Magazine* and the other in the *United Services Journal* in which is reported the discussion that took place upon it. As Brooman says, you must claim for the details. All is not lost yet. I now remember how careful I was in recommending a Patent Agent for fear that there might be any hitch. I thought best that you might continue to employ your own, more especially as they had the commission of the *Mechanics Magazine* but I did not know at that time which, though you afterwards wrote to me that they had been the means of losing you one Patent. I hope you have an agreement with Payne as to the foreign patents.

'Referring to your kind expressions and any interest I have taken in the matter, I must say that you are the most likely man I have ever known to bear another in mind in case of success, but with regard to others my experience suggests to me painful memories.

'My sea water project will be I think a success. I hope to start about April with a small limited Company. Glaisher and Le Feuvre join me.

'My wife joins in her regard to you and your wife. Lily is at school. I heard with sorrow about your head. I have a friend suffering from the same.'

Stringfellow was still afflicted with 'neuralgia in his head' causing him to wear a woollen knitted cap more often than a formal hat, and his eyesight had long necessitated wearing spectacles for detailed work, but his interest remained as keen as ever.

The reference to the sea water project has not been elucidated, but it may have been a proposed method of propulsion for ships using a fish-like tail. Brearey's partner, James Glaisher, as superintendent of the Meteorological Department at Greenwich, may have advised on the motion of waves, though his more spectacular specialisation had been investigation of the higher strata of the atmosphere, for which purpose he had made outstanding balloon flights with Henry Coxwell eight years earlier, achieving the then stupendous altitude of 37,300 feet. The maritime connection of Mr Le Feuvre was more obvious. Known as George Shaw Le Feuvre, he had been elected as Member of Parliament for Reading in 1863 and in 1866 was appointed Civil Lord of the Admiralty. Ultimately he was raised to the Peerage as Baron Eversley of Old Ford.

Nothing is known of Stringfellow's activities during the next four months except that he had been far from well. But on 15 June

Brearey wrote: 'My wife and I were a little amused at your saying that you were not worse after your Turkish Bath! It is not a very hopeful cure under such circumstances I am sorry to think, but I hope this warm weather will have done something for you.

'I wrote to Marriott and in return received the enclosed, but no letter. I suspect that he did not want to say anything about you. I send you his *News Letter* which you can keep. Also the report of the Aerial Steam Navigation Co. which you must please return to me. What is that round thing at the base of his plane?

'We shall have another meeting on 13 July. Several enquired of you at the last meeting as to how you were getting on. I wish we could have a day together at Seaton this hot weather. The sea water scheme is all right, but the delays are most annoying.

'Lily said this morning, getting dressed: "It is very strange Mrs Stringfellow does not write", at which I laughed and said "Suppose you had a letter this morning, then Mrs Stringfellow would say on Friday morning that it was very strange that Lily does not write, so every three days there would be letter writing!"

'My wife desires me to give her kind love to Mrs Stringfellow and says she wishes she could write everything that would interest her.'

Exactly a month later Brearey wrote: 'I send you two more numbers of the *News Letter* which you need not return. Marriott has not otherwise replied to me, but I had a letter from a member in India yesterday to whom he had replied in a letter dated 5 April, and the Member sent me a copy of it. He says: "You can go above the current of air, or you can skim as a partridge does over a corn field just high enough to be removed from the surrounding objects. Our experimental engine is not equal to ¼ horse-power. I call it a bat-power, and yet it also went against a strong current of air ruffling the waters of the lakes around Shellmound Park. The whole thing has now resolved itself into engine power alone, and as all the specific gravity should be balanced by the lifting power of the hydrogen gas we cannot discover a doubting point. I omitted to say we have now ready a 5 hp engine and boiler with water and fuel weighing only 364 lbs. When things are ready for starting the machine you can have some idea of the force of speed by keeping an eye to the shape and planes of the vehicle".'

That apparently refers to the trial of a machine based on Marriott's patent, which Brearey thought must be of particular interest to his friend. This led him to ask: 'Who is that Henson who advertises as a Civil Engineer in the News Letter?'. Then he inconsequentially adds: 'It seems very strange about the Great Seal. I cannot understand it. Is there no one attending to your Patent abroad?

'I saw Professor Pepper of the Polytechnic the other day. He much wishes to explain something connected with aerial navigation and talked of going down to see you. Could we get up a lecture?'

John Henry Pepper was a forty-nine year-old chemist who had been appointed lecturer at The School of Medicine and at the Royal Polytechnic. He had written a series of science manuals which gained wide circulation, but he was best known for an apparatus producing spectral optical illusion. Though aerial navigation was the ostensible subject of discussion he would also have been welcome at Chard because of Stringfellow's interest in medical matters, as exemplified by his scarificator and electrical treatment, and there would be mutual interest in optics because of Stringfellow's photographic specialisation.

It seems that Brearey visited Stringfellow during that summer and early autumn, for on 30 September he warns: 'I write at once to stop you sending any apples, for I see what you are after! I had a recollection of being on a roadside with you where there were a lot of apples and I thought them so cheap that I wanted to compare the price per bushel with those in this neighbourhood, and if there was any material difference to have up a bushel or two, but if I have them I shall insist on paying for them, for with all the claims upon you and losses, you cannot afford to keep up your subscription to the Society, so you had better send me a notice of withdrawal before the subscription should become due next month.'

He next expresses sympathy for Frederick John Stringfellow, who had apparently encountered a disaster. The letter continues: 'I am very sorry to hear about Fred. This is a sad thing. Surely they could set up a subscription for him? You seem to be getting quite celebrated for light engines. Could you set Edward to work?'

The subject then apparently changes to sales promotion of the armoured vehicle: 'If that £10,000 did not hinder Payne, then it would be something else. However I am in negotiation with a man. If you like I will send Lord Westbury the four reports. Is it "Hinton House near Crewkerne"?'

They were aiming high, for seventy year-old Baron Westbury, a famous barrister, was Lord Chancellor.

There was also the question of supplying a small steam engine to drive the fan of a modest 10 foot long wind tunnel which the Aeronautical Society had authorised Wenham to build for measurements of pressures on flat surfaces at various angles to the wind. Stringfellow used the new Post Office Telegram service on 16 November to contact Brearey, who replied: 'I received your Telegram at 2.50 p.m. I enclose it as a specimen! I gathered from my own judgement that it was half done, but of course where the object is *immediate*, time is the principal factor and he would require a certain time fixed for completion. I got estimates from Olrick and Wenham, and sent them the day after the letter appeared. I thought of you a hundred times but gave up the idea because I did not know that you were so far advanced, and I knew that you would require much time. Wenham will complete one of 5 hp in six weeks, weight under 700 lbs, for £250. However I suspect there will be more inquiries, so give me all particulars and get on with it.'

Chapter 10

A Wonderful Old Gentleman

Inevitably it was the subject of flying machines to which Brearey returned in his next letter of 18 February 1871: 'I have not been unmindful of the questions which you wished me to put to the Experimental Committee. They met last Thursday. Mr Young, whose letter I enclose, made experiments which entitle him to an opinion. Mr Wenham had previously told me that judging from those experiments, the speed of your model should be 25 mph, but as to the thrust of the screw he said that was the very question which the Committee was formed to discover. Please return Mr Young's letter. Edward had better take a copy.

'I don't think I told you that your subscription was due the 13th November — not that I am in any hurry for it. I hope this nice mild weather will do you good. My wife desires her kind love to Mrs Stringfellow. Lily is at school. How does Laura get on? I am afraid Edward's arm will always be weak.'

Twenty-six year-old Edward was the Stringfellows' photographer son who had returned from America and joined the army, but was injured when thrown by his horse.

There are no surviving letters for the next seven months, though correspondence must have continued. Meanwhile the Franco/Prussian War had come to an end. On 26 February the preliminaries of peace were signed, France agreeing to cede Alsace and German Lorraine, including Metz, to Germany and to pay an indemnity of five million francs. To emphasise the victory a large body of German troops marched across the Seine, passed under the Arc de Triomphe and down the Champs Elysee — but in accordance with an express stipulation they evacuated Paris next day, and a new chapter of the history of Europe began.

The German successes and exhaustion of France caused the British army to consider their lack of preparation had this country to face German forces on English soil. Mr Disraeli made mockery of the 'attenuated armaments' to which, he said, the Liberal Government had reduced the military strength. Estimates were presented to Parliament for increased expenditure of the fighting department. John Stringfellow hoped that would give opportunity of selling his armoured vehicle. But there was immediate outcry at the £2,700,000 that the Chancellor of the Exchequer would have to raise for military purposes by additional duties on wills, income tax, and above all by a tax on matches. A procession of matchmakers a thousand strong marched from Bethnal Green to Westminster to protest, and the tax was withdrawn.

On 21 March public attention switched to the marriage of Her Majesty's fourth daughter, Princess Louise to the Marquis of Lorne — the first time since the Royal Marriage Act of 1772 that a descendant of George II had married a Commoner with consent of the reigning Sovereign. As always on these royal occasions opportunity was taken for a gala day in England's towns and villages and Chard was no exception. Of John Stringfellow's activities there is little information, but Arthur Howell's diary of 7 June 1871 states: 'I at Chard met Mr Stringfellow.' And again on 11 June: 'Mr Stringfellow here . . . . brought me up three likenesses.'

In the autumn there was a visit from Brearey, and on 3 October he wrote: 'It rained when I parted from you. It rained all day and has rained more or less ever since, so I was forced to congratulate myself upon my being mildewed at home instead of at Chard! Today it is beautiful. I have now a special object in writing to you. You perhaps may remember a Mr Harte who wrote a pamphlet which he sent to all our members? I went to see him yesterday at his request and thought I saw an opening for some almost immediate result. He has constructed an aerial machine, the photograph of which he showed me. Dimensions as follows: Each wing 21 feet, space between for himself 1½ feet, therefore from tip to tip 43½ feet; surface 300 sq ft; weight about 73 lbs — so that there is sufficient surface to carry himself and a steam engine, for he is a small but muscular man.

'He begged me to write and ask you if you would grant him an interview and show him the action of your screws, for hitherto he has moved the wings by his manual power — not quite satisfactory. It is almost a certainty that if that engine were finished you might have a good return from it. If your reply is favourable he will go to Chard to see you. Tell Ed from me I hope he will take a spurt at the engine and work it right off.

'There is a capital article in the *Cornhill Magazine* for October. If you cannot see it, let me know and I will lend it to you. Kind regards to you all from self and wife.'

There must have been an intermediate letter from Stringfellow for on 7 October 1871 Brearey wrote: 'I am very sorry that you think it necessary to complete the engine before you see Mr Harte. In my opinion it is easy to imagine what an engine of a certain horse power and weight will do, but I am afraid that he will be ordered abroad by his Physician for the winter, and he would have seen you before he went; or as he told me, he would give up going abroad in spite of the Doctors if you and he could come to some arrangement.'

On 12 October he wrote again: 'I have had a very nice letter from Mr Harte this morning. You will find him a very nice young fellow. He is desirous of doing anything you may propose, and there need be no difficulty. He says that his Patent is nothing, and that he would pay more than it cost. He hopes to see you he says on Friday or Saturday. I fancy he has means at command which I trust will hasten the conjunction of his plane surface and your steam power, equal to the support of man and machine.'

Brearey then mentions Camille Vert, builder of the steam engine exhibited at the Crystal Palace as a rival to Stringfellow: 'Vert's boiler, which I fancy was made upon your principle, was applied to the propulsion of a balloon in Paris, and exploded — but harmlessly!'

December brought a letter from Brearey saying: 'I have sold your little card cure for £1-1s and shall shortly be paid for it I suppose. At any rate you may debit me with the amount. Lily was much pleased with the knife. I am almost afraid that while I write, you may be mourning, for I was much grieved to hear about your son, Tom, and fear worse news.

'We have tried our experiments at Perises, but they are not yet tabulated. This much only I know for certainty, that at 45° a surface exposed to the wind has under all circumstances the direct pressure and the lifting pressure exactly equal. I must go and see how Spencer is getting on.

'Shill (partner of Moy) has become a member this week. He and Moy are very busy at something. You should see Pettigrew's last work in which there is a picture of your Aerial Machine. I can lend it you if you won't keep it long, as there are others of our members who want it.

'My wife is away from me for a month in Essex. Kind regards to yours.'

That December the Stringfellows' fifth son, Thomas George, a jeweller at Taunton, died at the age of thirty two.

*   *   *

The year 1872 was characterised by extreme atmospheric activity. January was ushered in by heavy and disastrous floods, followed in the summer by thunderstorms of unprecedented severity and frequency which stripped forests of their trees and flooded low-lying villages, and the closing months witnessed several hurricanes which caused extensive destruction to shipping.

There was also widespread unrest among agricultural labour-
ers, particularly those of Dorset, Somerset and Devon. In
Somerset, wages in the western districts were 7s or 8s a week,
with 2 or 3 pints of cider a day as a perk, valued at 1s. Sometimes
grist corn and potatoes were given, but in Dorset a labourer's
cottage was often rent free and the pay only 2s a week. Though in
the north conditions were much better with wages from 15s to 18s
a week, seventy per cent of the Somerset population were
paupers. Nevertheless Chard remained reasonably flourishing
because of the lace industry.

No Stringfellow letters survive from this period, but undoubtedly correspondence was maintained with Brearey. Certainly the Aeronautical Society was continuing its scientific
investigations under the direction of Wenham, and a model was
also built by Shill and Moy of their proposed Aerial Steamer
driven by multi-blade screws from a 3 hp steam engine.

However the next surviving letter from Brearey was 15 January
1873. Five days earlier Napoleon III had died at Chislehurst,
Kent, but that caused no considerable sensation and France
received the news with profound indifference.

Brearey wrote: 'I enclose receipt for your subscription with
thanks. My Vienna correspondent, Mr Michael (a member) sent
me his photo with a request for mine. His photo is not only the
best I ever saw but it is that of the handsomest man I ever saw,
and I wanted to send him one of mine. I could not however send
one of those you sent me, though you must have had much
trouble with them and I felt you ought to be paid for them, but
your Yorkshire sense of independence won't allow you to accept
payment unless you are satisfied with the work done. Nevertheless what would you charge anybody else? I must get a negative
taken here in the first style of Art, in return for his.

'Hall seems to be spending a lot of money over his Aerial
machine, but he meets with the difficulty of which all amateurs
complain, viz to find workmen to comprehend, and work to, his
orders. He never went to Dunrobin. He can work himself and
wants a place less distant. Could he make an arrangement with
you for the use of your workshop? I think he would be glad. A
Happy New Year to you and continuing health. I notice you don't
complain on that score.'

Again there is a lapse of Brearey letters for over two years.
Much was happening. The war in Ashantee, bordering the
African Gold Coast, was sporadically waged from the summer of
1873, but was successfully concluded in February 1874. That
same month, to Stringfellow's dismay as a Liberal, the ebullient
Tory Mr Disraeli ousted Mr Gladstone as Prime Minister. Among

the many problems that spring was famine in Bengal, and there were domestic issues such as the Scottish Patronage Bill and the Public Worship Regulation Act giving parishioners power to prosecute clergymen who introduced practices not in accordance with ritual. The textile industry also came under review and working hours were reduced from sixty to fifty-seven a week, and the minimum age of juvenile operatives was raised to ten. At Chard the lace-factory workers at last managed to set up a local Lodge of the Amalgamated Society of Operative Lace Makers, and Stringfellow felt this could be the beginning of trouble.

With the opening of 1875 Mr Gladstone announced that he had determined to resign leadership of the Liberal Party. The Queen's Speech of 6 February ushered no sensational sessions. My Lords and Gentlemen were informed that the peace of Europe had remained unbroken; that the question of formally recognising King Alfonso was under consideration; there was an improved state of affairs on the Gold Coast; and measures for better government of Natal, the annexation of Fiji, and the restoration of prosperity to the provinces of India. All received favourable comments.

On 22 April 1875 Brearey wrote to Stringfellow (changing emphasis from the formal 'My dear Sir' to the affectionate 'My dear Friend'): 'It seems a long time since I held communication with you. I was looking over your last letter this morning while arranging my correspondence, and you had then returned to your old love. I am like a flooded mine and take a deal of pumping before anything can be got out of me, so I cannot relate all that is doing in aeronautics. It seems a relief to write upon some other subject. Sufficient that Moy is still going on experimenting at the Crystal Palace. They were unable to get the machine to run along the ground around the central fountain at more than 12 mph by means of the aerial screw wheels when 25 mph was wanted before it should float off the ground.

'Just as they had got to this point two months ago, whilst coming home from the Crystal Palace about 7 pm, our carriage had a collision on the roadway and I was knocked on the head insensible. I was in bed a month and there are injuries to both knees which prevent me from taking exercise, so that my head does not have the chance which it might have. This is the tenth week since it happened and we want to know how you and yours are.

'I ought to add that Moy hopes to rise vertically with the new arrangement he has just completed. He and Shill have spent about £3,000 on this.'

But alas for such hopes. Moy's machine was an impracticable device for which he had been granted Patent 8238, and comprised tandem low aspect ratio wings of a mere 50 sq ft forward and 64 sq ft aft, between which were two side-by-side huge six-bladed propelling devices of 160 sq ft total surface slatted like a windmill.

By the late summer John Stringfellow had been induced to visit London, and on 8 September Brearey wrote: 'Let me know what time your train arrives at Waterloo so that I may be able to calculate what hour I may meet you at Greenwich Station. They leave Waterloo for Greenwich every 20 minutes, starting from Charing Cross at the hour. We have got bed and board at the house, small as it is, and a hearty welcome. I expect Bennett on Monday and we will have Moy too. Very kind regards to your wife. My wife and Lily also send kind messages to your wife.'

Again there was a long gap in surviving correspondence. John Stringfellow at 76 years old was taking things quietly. He followed the general public's interest in Disraeli's proposal to buy the Khedive's share of the Suez Canal for £4,000,000 as unanimously sanctioned by the House of Commons. There had also been a much publicised visit of the Prince of Wales to the Indian Princes, and subsequently the Additional Titles Bill was passed by Disraeli in 1876 giving the Queen authority to assume the title of Empress of India.

But it is not until 1877, the year in which Stringfellow's youngest daughter Laura died, that the Brearey correspondence continues on 27 January, written in less firm hand: 'The time is coming when I must start on my lecture tour. My first is Liskeard on Tuesday the 6th February. If you and your wife are well enough and others matters agreeable, I should like to come to you on Friday 2nd February and leave you for Liskeard on Tuesday morning. Then I lecture at Plymouth, Wednesday: Redruth, Thursday; Truro, Friday; Penzance, Monday; Leeds, Wednesday; Keighley, Saturday. In the meantime every moment is occupied, so farewell.'

These days he was making a succession of lecture tours on behalf of the Aeronautical Society and on 29 December 1877 wrote to Stringfellow: 'I last heard from you just previous to my journey northward, I had a very successful tour, gratifying in every respect. Cutlers Hall was full to overflowing, but I suppose you would see the Sheffield papers. The best report that I have yet had was at Grimsby where the audience was really enthusiastic. I had one clear day in Edinburgh and a most lovely day it was. You would hear that I called upon Mr Carter with whom I was much pleased. I stayed at the Cockburn Hotel and next morning went on to Falkirk where I had again a large audience of about 1,200. Next day I lectured at Linlithgow, about 7 miles off.

'Upon the whole, however, I was disappointed. I expected four times the number of engagements, and I think I have had only one more than the first year. However, in my next circular I shall be more of a showman and head it with a copy of a Photograph of all my models as arranged behind one on a screen when I lecture. There are more than 30, and make a good show from wings of 6 inches up to 12½ feet from tip to tip. I mounted the two crows wings which you sent me and I could even get it to fly a bit. I then ascertained that crow weighs about 17 ounces. I added a half pound to the weight and it flew 16 feet. I have not done with that gentleman yet, but when I have time, shall balance it better. That is what is wanted besides giving it a little more stroke of wing. What should you think a crow's wing describes at the tips? I want some more crows' wings. The Duke of Sutherland, our Chairman, is going to send me herons, gulls and hawks.'

It is interesting that Stringfellow's advice was still being sought. On 31 March of the following year Brearey wrote: 'Many thanks for remembrance of me. I received the four crows in beautiful condition. I must cut off the wings and tails and dry them for future experiments. I am glad to hear how well you have got over the winter, but it is just now most trying weather and great caution is required. I am so busy that I have no spare time, but if you take the *English Mechanic* you will see in February 8, March 8 and 22nd, what has been said about my models and lectures. I have arranged with Mr Browning, the mathematical instrument maker in the Strand, to sell models at 1s/6d each and advertise them. My wife makes the wings. I get brasswork fitted onto the shaft all complete for 2s/6d. I have made some very diminutive models which will wind up nearly 200 times and fly beautifully. I showed the models to Browning who at once ordered a dozen.

'I am afraid it is impossible to work the machinery inside a rook. How beautifully you have skinned that specimen. The rooks you sent me weigh 1¼ lbs, and have a 152 sq ins of wing.'

The next paragraph shows that Stringfellow was regarded as the expert on Cayley.

'Are there any more of Sir George Cayley's papers that should be published? I want the matter for the next Report.

'I have nothing doing down your way. My next lecture is at Birmingham April 23 and my last engagement this season. We all join in kind love to you both, and hope to see you in the spring, or rather in early summer.'

But later that year the optimism had gone, for on 16 December Brearey wrote: 'I have not much heart for correspondence. My wife lies seriously ill. I may be too despondent although that is not usual for me, but I dread the worst. Some internal disease to which the doctor cannot yet give a name. God's will be done, and this is all I dare say at the present moment. However, I suppose I must attend to the business of the Society whatever takes place. Your subscription of one guinea fell due November 13.

'I hope you and your wife are well this severe weather. I lectured at Rotherham on Thursday last and came back on Saturday, staying in Sheffield two days with my cousin who is a surgeon there. I lately passed through Edinburgh twice on my way to Peterhead and Peebles. I still go on experimenting, and I made a kite 10 ft long fly by a wave-like action from stem to stern — but life is not long enough as you know yourself. I should have liked your nephew to have heard what I had to say about you in my lecture. Lily is a very attentive nurse. She sends her love to you both.'

*   *   *

In 1879 Fred Brearey patented his undulating method of propulsion based on observations of a swimming fish. The Specification (No 2376) stated:

> 'An elongated body pointed at both ends contains the requisite machinery and the passengers. Flexible lever-arms extend on either side, and a flexible spar extends from the tail end of the body. Silk or other suitable fabric is extended from the arms and along the spar of the tail, thus giving a large supporting surface, and vibrations are imparted to the area which propels the machine by a wave-like motion.'

On 26 April 1880 Brearey wrote encouragingly to Stringfellow: 'My dear old Friend — all my investigations into the subject of light boilers have resulted in confirming my original opinion, viz there is yet nothing equal to yours. Can you put me in the way of having one made for some 5 or 6 hp? I have your drawings for a 4 hp. Has your son Fred completed his? If I recollect right, you said the whole thing, engine and all, would be made under 40 lbs weight. I think that Fred has greatly exceeded this.

'When can you and your wife pay us a visit? Please reply to these enquiries as soon as you can.'

The reply has not been found, but on 24 November Brearey wrote with the usual request: 'I make to you my annual application for your guinea subscription in aid of the Aeronautical Society, but I would favour your desire if you wish to sever connection with the Society, for I dare say you are heartily sick of the stagnation which, for want of a golden spoon to stir us up, seems to have settled upon us. Judging from my correspondence at home and abroad there is no lack of interest in the subject of aerial navigation. The late discussion in the *English Mechanic* proves this.'

Indeed aerial navigation appeared to be in the doldrums, discouragement having quenched the first fine enthusiasms, though Brearey himself was hopeful that his experiments in wave-motion wings might afford a practical solution — but his single-mindedness as an active experimenter led him into trouble with other members. As he explained to John Stringfellow in that same letter of 24 November: 'Until I made what I thought to be a discovery, I was in ignorance of the nasty feeling excited by some workers at the presumption of any upstart contending for a place. Your son Frederick has written me a letter which has personally astonished me. His jealousy was excited on your behalf simply because I said that I was experimenting more than any other man. And so I am and cannot help myself, because lecturing as I do, I must show something demonstrative, and I am constantly at it; so I cannot be boasting when I state a simple fact that I am the only man who is making anything out of aeronautics, or rather I should say "Aerial Navigation". But as I am paid for lecturing, this is the case and naturally leads me up to the other — viz constant experiment. I have nothing else to do, living in a measure independently of other work.'

Correspondence continued in the following year, but none is extant though it is clear that Brearey was having problems with the patent rights of his flying machine and was diligent in keeping the old pioneer informed of the problems. On 7 December 1881 he wrote: 'Your mention of Mackenzie urges me to send you my printed defence. He has behaved like a fool and a good deal like a blackguard in as much as he has tried all he knows to ruin me with the Council by sending his written complaints containing incorrect statements. But I stood too high with the Council for a nameless sneak like him to harm me, and they have one and all declined to interfere in the matter.'

It seems that Mackenzie had invested in development of the wave-motion flying machine in expectation of early financial return, but more money was now required, which he refused to provide and instead was maligning Brearey to the Council. Probably the problem, common to all nineteenth century inventors, was the difficulty of obtaining light-weight power. Brearey told Stringfellow: 'I know of nothing but yours that would give me a few minutes trial. The question is how, without wasting money, to go about the manufacturing of an engine that would develop 2 hp? Would you superintend it, and for what remuneration if I sent down a competent person to work under your superintendance?

'I exhibited my wave model to Dr Petigrew some months ago at the Greenwich Lecture Hall. He was very much pleased, and acknowledged to the two young Misses Glaisher who were present that I was entitled to the discovery. Yet after he got home he wrote to me a long letter claiming it as his own, though he said in that letter "I acknowledge that you have successfully demonstrated flight by wave action".'

Brearey then explains to Stringfellow the proposed method of launching his flying machine down a steep gradient using a truck with large front wheels and small back ones in order to keep the platform horizontal — an echo of the method devised by Henson and Stringfellow for their *Ariel* of old. His letter continues: 'I have just obtained flight by another action quite novel, carrying a ¾ lb weight. I have shown flight in so many ways that my confidence has increased wonderfully, and if that damned fool Mackenzie had worked with me instead of against me, something might have been shown — but no sooner had the fool taken a share in the patents than he left for America and fully expected a fortune without doing a hand's turn to help me. I assure you I expect no fortune but I will accept all the assistance offered me by all those who do, for I have spent 17 years of my life in devotion to the interests of the science.'

His final reference to John Stringfellow is evocative: 'And now about yourself my friend. You are a most wonderful old gentleman. Letting alone yesterday being your 82nd birthday, you have survived numerous accidents and can bear being pitched into the road from a pony trap that gets smashed in the operation and yet live to describe the event. Your wife must be quite proud of her old Gentleman. But there is a good deal of kick left yet, and I am very glad to find that you are still hankering after realising the old dream — but I don't agree with you as to gas.'

This last reference indicates Stringfellow's life-long interest in engines and probably has reference to the fact that in 1876 the German engineer Otto had devised the compression-cycle engine which would presently lead to the petrol combustion engine and open a great vista of future transport. Apparently Stringfellow was still co-operating with his son Frederick over development of a biplane flying model, though it is improbable that he would have attempted to power it with a gas engine. At eighty-two he was more likely to have been pottering about and letting time drift by, no longer concerned with the politics of the day, such as Irish defiance of Whig and Tory alike, or the insurrection in Egypt, where England temporarily assumed the Protectorate in 1883.

Later that year John Stringfellow told his air-minded dentist son

John Stringfellow at seventy-five.

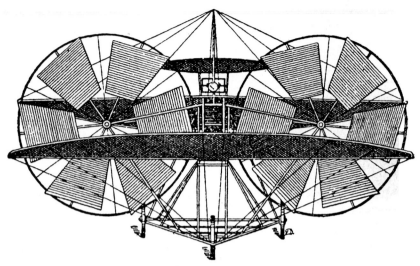

Thomas Moy's full-size Aerial Steamer, 1875.

Frederick Brearey's ripple-wing monoplane model.

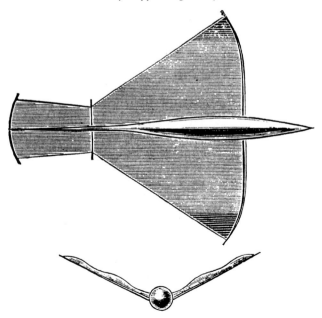

John Stringfellow's house in Chard, marked with a commemorative plate.

Hannah Stringfellow,
wife of John Stringfellow.

Frederick John Stringfellow's version of his father's model biplane. Crewkerne, 1886.

A rebuild of the 1868 triplane in the Smithsonian Museum, Washington D.C.

The first version of Frederick Stringfellow's 'quintuplane', in the garden of Candle Cottage.

Candle Cottage, Crewkerne, the home of Frederick John Stringfellow.

The Alexandra Palace Exhibition, with the second version of Stringfellow's quintuplane in the right foreground. Early wings and propellers can be seen in the left foreground.

Frederick John Stringfellow in his Masonic regalia.

The memorial to John Stringfellow, who died on 13 December 1883.

that the work he was executing for the improvement of his biplane was a mistake, and said, 'I have hung it up Fred. I shall touch it no more. I hope I have not spoiled it for you.'

On 12 September Brearey wrote to Frederick John Stringfellow with whom he maintained mutual interest not only in subjects related to air navigation but also horticulture: 'My dear Fred — I am glad to hear from you. You smell of Ferns. The Osmundas are still flourishing and have never been re-potted since I brought them home.

'Poor father! So he can do no more. Years ago, I was urgently wanting light motive power and could have paid for it, but I could not arrange anything satisfactory with your father. I even offered to send down a skilled workman if he would superintend him, but he never gave me even a reply. But you and I both know how the workman's tools would have been snatched out of his hands and he would have had nothing to do while your father worked.

'Now then as to this Engine and boiler? You must draw up full particulars as to the power which he hoped to obtain with the minimum of weight and I will insert an Advertisement in the Report which is in the Printer's hand. I have frequent enquiries from all parts of the world respecting the engine which gained our £100 prize. Could they have been manufactured, many would have been sold; but I soon learned the futility of applying to your father. No doubt a suitable advertisement will obtain notice. You must mention price and state distinctly what can be done.

'For my purpose I expect the Engine would be no use as it was intended no doubt to revolve a screw. I want a simple piston action because, whatever you may think, wing-wave action is a success and I have lately patented in France and America a superposed action. Having obtained the true proportion of parts, my models act well.'

That was the end. Three months later, on 13 December 1883, in the forty-sixth year of Queen Victoria's reign, John Stringfellow died.

Chapter 11
His Son Continues the Quest

The Chard and Ilminster News of 15 December 1883 gave John Stringfellow an affectionate obituary, extolling his 'large general knowledge of men and things, a wonderous memory, and a mind well stored and cultured which helped to render Mr Stringfellow so genial and attractive in society', but could not forbear mentioning that though he was a member of the Baptist Church 'the Vicar of the Borough's St Mary's Church officiated though the interment was on the non-conformist ground of the Town Cemetery, thus exhibiting a degree of Christian morality not often to be found even in these days'.

The newspaper account confirmed that: 'Mr Stringfellow, about sixty years ago, came from Nottingham to Chard by the invitation of some that wished to secure the advantage of his known skill as a Bobbin and Carriage manufacturer, which business he had learned at Nottingham. Although then a young man of only about twenty, he gave proof of his ability by some important improvements which he introduced in this special branch of manufacture, having previously expressed his disgust with the style of work as he found it. For sometime after his settlement at Chard he supplied one or more of our factories, and subsequently set up strictly on his own account in High Street, on the site where formerly stood the Friends' Meeting House. In 1833 he bought the row of houses, of which his dwelling forms one, rebuilding this to make it available for his extended business. This branch of manufacture he continued to carry on until recently, sustaining his reputation for superior work up to the last, in proof of which we may mention that a skilled workman was about two years ago sent by Messrs Heathcote of Tiverton to work under him with a view, if possible, to emulate his skill.

'Amidst the activity involved in all this, Mr Stringfellow found time for many other pursuits, among which the most important and absorbing was the invention and perfecting of his aerial machine. He early became possessed of a strong faith, which nothing has shaken, that some method would be found of navigating the air, and he had an equally strong conviction that he could do it. To verify this belief became henceforth his strongest ambition, and in effect the great aim of his life to which personal comfort, success in business, and to an extent even home life, were subordinated. Only his nearest friends can form any conception of the sacrifice of time, money, self-interest and comfort, involved in the prosecutions of the cherished purpose through a long series of years against formidable odds, and amidst difficulties and discouragements which would have utterly crushed a weaker faith and less brave heart than his. Many will remember the fact of his spending weeks on Baaley Down where he had fixed a tent which served as workshop by day and sleeping apartment by night. Here he was able to carry on his experiments without the interruptions he must have experienced in the town.'

It is indicative that though this gossip-making event had long been remembered by Chard, there was no mention of Henson's association. That had ended thirty-five years ago when he vanished from the scene, yet John Stringfellow was still referred to by young and old as the 'flying man'.

The obituary commented that the Aeronautical Society's Exhibition of 1868 'had been the means of bringing Mr Stringfellow and his machine into notice. What measures of success would have been achieved with improved facilities, more time and practical help from the Government, is impossible to say. One thing is certain: that the highest credit is due to Mr Stringfellow, and much also of the credit given to others who have only embodied ideas originated by him. We are pleased to hear that there is yet a possibility of the work which he began and so enthusiastically prosecuted even to the last, being carried on and perfected. One of his sons (Mr F. J. Stringfellow), who seems to inherit much of his father's mechanical skill, if not his genius, will be engaged in completing some unfinished designs, and may thus succeed in accomplishing that which to his father was a matter only of fond anticipation and hope.' This would be the new biplane and steam power plant on which John Stringfellow had been slowly working, occasionally helped by that son.

Stringfellow's will, dated 19 February 1879, in which he describes himself as 'Engineer', opens with the bequest of all his furniture and household goods to his wife, and in the fifth line proceeds to: 'The models and machines for which I obtained a prize from the Aeronautical Society of Great Britain and known as "The Crystal Palace Models" with all the belongings, I give to my son Frederick John. The models and machinery made for use during the siege of Paris and known as "The Paris Models", with all the belongings, I give to my son Allen Harrison. All my other models, machines, machinery, tools and fittings I direct my Trustees to offer for sale to such of my children as may be desirous to purchase the same.' Instead they remained stored for years.

Stringfellow's friends Francis Mitchel the brewer and John Bath the Bank manager were the trustees and ensured that the widowed Hannah was reasonably provided for by 'the interest, dividend, and annual income' from her husband's trust monies, stocks, funds and securities.

When her son Allen moved into the family home, Frederick took Hannah under his care in Candle Cottage at Crewkerne. Some of her grandchildren who were contacted in the 1950s remembered her as a gracious lady sitting in her armchair in the front room there. Though several of Frederick John's children were by that time grown up and had left home, or died, the so-called cottage must have been very crowded, for the twelfth child, Valentine Bertram Turner Stringfellow, was only six years old and there had been three more since; but Valentine would briefly feature in the later phase of the Stringfellow saga.

*   *   *

The year after John Stringfellow's death the third great Parliamentary Reform Act added two million voters to the electorate, echoing the battle for reform in which John Stringfellow and his friends had so vigorously campaigned at Chard in earlier times. In that year Brearey wrote a Memoir of him which was published in the eighteenth Report of the Aeronautical Society for 1884, but contributed little new information other than a summation of what the author had gleaned in conversation with his old friend. At best, almost all that Brearey wrote was based on the fallible recollections of Stringfellow in old age and is not necessarily verbatim. Nor did he re-affirm the statement he had made sixteen years earlier in the *Popular Science Review* that Stringfellow had been engaged in experimenting with a view to constructing a machine large enough to carry a person to guide it. Even his conclusion was less than generous, but as Secretary of the Aeronautical Society he had to be careful not to offend the many other members who, like Thomas Moy, thought that they had the solution to this still unaccomplished subject of aerial navigation. So Brearey ended his Memoir: 'We who survive to pass judgement upon the results of a man's life should be very careful how we exercise that judgement. It is much too solemn a retrospect for the toleration of a flippant analysis. All that we are justified in concluding is that John Stringfellow considered that Aerial Navigation was capable of accomplishment and that he gave much time and means to its elucidation. In future years when this end is accomplished — as it surely will — his name will be included in the Roll of Fame.'

In fact, Stringfellow will remain unique for all time in being the first man in the world to make a heavier-than-air winged machine fly with a self-contained engine, to which end he pioneered use of air-propellers instead of the 'wafting' wings advocated by Sir George Cayley, and he at least ensured that his machine was longitudinally stable and could be trimmed with an adjustable tail. He had no illusion that it was more than a beginning.

The Aeronautical Society had long known that Frederick John Stringfellow was continuing his father's work, as reflected by an invitation to test the biplane model in the Banqueting hall of the Alexandra Palace during the Aeronautical Society's Exhibition held there in 1885, but as he later explained: 'I could not afford to avail myself of the offer for want of means, having to look after business for bread and cheese.' The machine in fact was still incomplete, Fred having employed his limited spare time to make and test the steam engine and 16-cone copper boiler which gave over two square feet of effective heating surface, supplying steam at 100 lbs per sq ins to the 1 3/16 ins diameter cylinder. To those who saw the prototype of the biplane, with top wing spanning 10 ft and the lower 8ft 10ins, it must have seemed a mere flight of fancy, but the design would have been a forward-looking concept even among the aeroplanes of a quarter-century later.

There is no specific contemporary record of flying trials of this machine, yet unlikely that it was never tried or a failure, for in due course he built a multi-plane of very similar concept to compare the flying qualities. He also built a model on the plan of the 1848 one, but heavier and more powerful. That one or other flew is indicated by a letter received in 1972 from an 86 year-old lady, Mrs F S Hann: 'I wonder if you would be interested in a machine built by a Mr Stringfellow of Chard? I remember clearly being taken with the family by my father to see what he called "The Bird" flying machine. We saw it from between Mosterton and Misterton in Somerset flying over fields near Crewkerne like a huge bird. I am sorry that I can give no further details as I must have been quite small, but it was something always to remember.'

She must have meant Frederick John Stringfellow of Crewkerne, as endorsed by an old gravedigger there who told a later occupier of Candle Cottage that his late father had seen Frederick John flying his model on nearby Bincombe Hill.

But now in 1887 it was Queen Victoria's Jubilee on 21 June. Every city, town and village flaunted its flags and bunting. The Queen emerged from her long widowhood to attend a thanksgiving service in Westminster Abbey attended by a great assembly of European Monarchs, Princes, Indian potentates, and distinguished representatives of the colonies and dependencies. There were Triumphal arches at every corner of London's processional route, with grandstands lining thoroughfares crowded with legions of happy people, and until late at night vast multitudes walked streets ablaze with illuminations. On the Malvern Hills a huge beacon fire was lit at 10 pm as signal for similar fires on heights all over the kingdom.

'The enthusiastic reception,' wrote Her Majesty, 'has touched me deeply. It has shown that the labour and the anxiety of fifty long years, twenty-two of which I spent in unclouded happiness shared by my beloved husband, have been appreciated by my people.' Moreover, it had been fifty years of outstanding scientific, social and industrial development which embraced the dawn of the air navigation age as initiated by Sir George Cayley with his researches and John Stringfellow with the world's first powered flight.

Though the flight of Frederick's steam-powered, tractor model biplane derivative may not have been until 1888, that year had a more direct link with John Stringfellow because on 23 March the *Daily Advertiser* in Newark, New Jersey, reported that William Samuel Henson had died on the previous day at the age of seventy-six — but the news failed to filter through to England.

Henson's biographer, Paul Johnston, many years later conjectured that he was not essentially aeronautically minded, nor had he the scientific curiosity and educational background of a Sir George Cayley, but was primarily a mechanic and inventor.

Johnston said: 'Henson was certainly not one of the great men of history. He made little lasting contribution to science or engineering. He was one who let his imagination roam in regions which could not be explored and exploited until more solid workers contribed the tools to cut the steps on which to climb. Such Will-o'-the-wisps of science serve a useful purpose. They dart hither and yon, encouraging others to venture after them. Some of their followers stumble into pitfalls and vanish. Others find solid footing and win some lasting achievement.'

Thus it was Stringfellow who remained historically renowned for his aeronautical achievements not only in Chard but beyond, whereas Henson, his eager young pupil, had long been forgotten.

Even now no other inventor had achieved practical success with powered aeroplane flight, but the possibility of flying had become of widespread interest and hundreds of patents to that end had been granted, though to no avail. Yet the fame of Stringfellow had reached America where that eminent astronomer and researcher in astro-physics, the Secretary of the Smithsonian Institution, Samuel Pierpoint Langley, had begun to investigate the problems of mechanical flight in 1886, using a whirling arm to test the lift of inclined surfaces, much as John

Chapman had done for Henson forty years earlier. Seeking aid for his research, Langley had written to Frederick Stringfellow, and in February 1887 purchased from him both the prize-winning steam engine and the unique triplane which John Stringfellow had exhibited nineteen years earlier at the Aeronautical Society's Crystal Palace Exhibition, for he realised that a similar arrangement of twin propellers driven by a light steam engine was almost certainly the best way of powering the tandem-winged models that he had been developing using twisted-rubber power as devised by Stringfellow and Pénaud.

However, the Stringfellow triplane proved of no particular value to Langley because his experiments were leading in a different direction. In any case the model had deteriorated so much in storage and transit that in March 1889 he presented it to the Smithsonian Museum where it was rebuilt by M Vaniman, who six years later patented an impractical 'Aerial machine without aerostats' comprising framework carrying large opposite rotating propellers either side surmounted by a shed-like roof twice as long as it was wide. The Vaniman rebuild of the Stringfellow triplane, despite use of original parts, differed considerably from the photograph which has always been regarded as that of the original model, but the latter may have been modified by Stringfellow's son to give the tail surface arrangement and smaller forward triangular surface of the re-build, which also has inappropriate larger propellers sent by Fred Stringfellow. Both models differ in propeller location from the not necessarily correct artist's drawing of the 1868 Exhibition, though this may imply that John Stringfellow continued to experiment. However, having had the inspirational benefit of dismantling and detailed inspection of the prize engine, Langley rather pompously dismissed it as unlikely to given even one-tenth of the alleged 1 hp!

Correspondence with him may well have caused Fred Stringfellow to reconsider the structural advantages of rectangular shaped wings and their consequent use for the five-winged multiplane he built of similar size to his swallow-winged biplane model, but apparently with deeper cabin lest the lower wing became injured when landing. Like the biplanes, the machine had a remarkably advanced appearance, employing a single bracing bay on each side, with wings progressively reduced in superposed span and separated by side-wall struts. Probably this was the machine which Mrs Hann eventually saw flying over the fields. It was still in existence, though in modified form, in 1903.

*   *   *

Meanwhile, Brearey had been maintaining correspondence with Frederick Stringfellow, and on 19 July 1988 wrote to him again on the subject of engines: 'My dear Fred — I would have given more than £25 for that Engine when I wrote to your father about it, for at that time I had the money. If it is in working order (about which you best know) and you will sell for £25 I would write once more to Mr Frost and offer it to him for that. He paid £100 for the one he ordered and which did not suit him after all, and he had a law suit about it which he won against Ahrbecker but never got his costs or any recompense.' E P Frost JP, was a hard-working member of the Society, but sufficiently misguided to concentrate on ornithopters for which he thought artificially feathered wings were essential!

Brearey's letter continued: 'We have a spare bed now which some of our friends take advantage of occasionally, and if it should be disengaged when you come to London you will be welcome to it. My wife sends her kind regards to you both.'

On 14 September he wrote again about the engine: 'There is a man wants one at this moment to whom I have sent your letter and spoke about your engines etc. He says write and tell him to bring it up with him. He will give it warehouse room. He says also he will help you to sell it, but he thinks he may want it himself. His workshop, a very large one, is close to me at Eastpoint Hill, Greenwich.

'I certainly hope you will continue to see me — by which expression I gather you are going to stay with some friends, but when you do come, let me know first and we can arrange a bed so that you need not be away in the evening and we can show you something worth showing.'

At about this time Frederick Stringfellow made the acquaintance through Brearey of Christopher H M Alderson, a friend of Thomas Moy, though a horticulturist by profession at Orpington, Kent, thus adding a mutuality of interest to Fred's hobby of flower growing. Friendship developed and it soon transpired that Alderson was fascinated with the idea of making a flying machine and to that end wanted a steam engine, whereupon Fred wrote to him on 30 October 1890 saying: 'I have sent you the first engine which was made for the first Aerial Steam Carriage. It is not as first made as the piston rod then worked both ends of the cylinder direct on the propellers, but the speed was not sufficient although this engine as it was then with 3 ft propellers at 60°s, gave 300 rpm and had a thrust of 5 lbs 4½ ozs at commencement and steady at 4 lbs 2 ozs, with steam at 100 lbs per sq ins.

'If I had a piece of brass, I would have made a new eccentric, but it works very well as it is, and the last time I tried it was perfectly steam tight at the above pressure. If you will accept it you are welcome as I have four other engines made, and you may amuse yourself with it.

'I was at Seaton last Thursday and saw the herons lazily sailing about above the salt marshes and really it seemed as if no exertion was required. I have done nothing the whole of the summer with the traps as I have been fairly busy otherwise, but if business gets slack and I have a little time to spare, I shall try a few experiments and I know one worked well last summer.

'As the stalk of the *Calla Eliotias* is dry I have enclosed the crown of seeds so you will be able, if of any use, to ripen them better than I can. My dahlias have been very good latterly. Starfish is a gem and many others of the new ones are good.'

That letter led to Alderson becoming a key factor in saving the historic collection of John Stringfellow's models, and his interest in aviation currently took more practical form through joining the Aeronautical Society. However, the slow advance of 'aerial navigation' remained handicapped by lack of a suitable power-plant, but the ex-patriot American engineer, Hiram Maxim — born at the time when Henson and Stringfellow were beginning to dream of a great aeroplane in 1840 — had decided, after investigation of the crude state of petroleum motors, to follow John Stringfellow's lead with steam for a flying machine and wrote to Frederick seeking information on his father's power plants, as well as maintaining correspondence with his fellow American, Langley, on the technical aspects of flight and steam power. Maxim's Patent No 16883 of 1889 reveals his proposals for a huge biplane equivalent of the 'Aerial Carriage' powered by two 180 hp steam engines, and at the Aeronautical Society's meeting in November 1891 he described his early aerodynamic experiments and the construction of this machine.

In 1892 Frederick Stringfellow, now 60 years old, published a booklet at Chard entitled *A Few Remarks on what has been done with Screw-Propelled Aeroplane Machines from 1809-1892*. Because he was only a boy when his father conducted those crucial early experiments leading to the first powered flight of a heavier-than-air machine and had subsequently been abroad from 1849 to late 1853 and then from 1854 to at least 1860, he largely copied Brearey's *Popular Science Revue* articles of 1869 and the latter's more recent *Memoir of John Stringfellow* of 1883 for information about his father, which at best was second hand. Nevertheless, when Frederick's booklet was published there were many people who still remembered the mature John Stringfellow, and those his son mentions as witnessing the 1848 flights did not demur at being named to that effect. Like his father, Frederick shunned publicity and did not mention his own continuing experiments, though photographs taken at Candle Cottage are clear evidence of his work.

Among other experimenters he briefly mentions Maxim, whom he trusts 'will solve in proper manner the problem which has been of such interest in all ages'.

The twin-engined central portion of Maxim's machine, temporarily fitted with an auxiliary aerofoil above the main area, was completed in 1893 and made several experimental runs along broad-gauge rails extending half a mile across Baldwyns Park in Kent where he had built a vast shed for it. Maxim published his initial results to date in the March 1893 issue of *Engineering* and subsequently more runs were made along the rails. One of these made on 12 September was described by an American correspondent: 'I mounted the platform made of light matchboard. . . A rope was pulled and the machine shot forward like a railway locomotive — and with the big wheels whirling, the steam hissing, and the waste pipes puffing and gurgling, flew over the 1,800 ft of track. It was stopped by a couple of ropes stretched across the track working on capstans fitted with a reverse fan. The stoppage was quite gentle. The ship was then pushed back over the track by the men.' Even the Prince of Wales' son, George was given a run.

Other people's success did not prevent Fred Stringfellow from continuing with his 'quintuplane', though it had become more of a hobby than scientific research. That there must have been flight trials is indicated by a later photograph showing a modified version with the original wing bay now divided by midway insertion of similarly surfaced I-struts to the originals.

He was also still involved with steam engines, and on 12 September 1893 Brearey wrote notifying that: 'A member in America wants an estimate for engine and boiler not exceeding 10 lbs per horse power. He will take one up to 25 hp. Can you do anything? These are separated enquiries now.'

That was followed eight days later with: 'My dear Fred — I have given your address to Mr McCormick. I think that he might be willing to work with you. You might benefit by the connection. He is very generous with his money.

'We were I assure you, quite moved to hear your troubles. Lily desired me to say how she sympathised. Even her life is not all beer and skittles.'

Correspondence continued with Brearey and other members of the Aeronautical Society, including Major B F S Baden-Powell to whom Frederick wrote on 8 February 1894: 'I have for disposal a much larger engine with two cylinders 2½ or 3 inch diameter with copper boiler cones.' This was the engine intended for the Paris Siege dirigible, and seemed a possible power unit to prolong the flight of a small glider which Baden-Powell was building — but he did not buy it.

Later that year the full span outboard and lower wings were fitted to Maxim's machine, and precautionary rails were mounted a few inches above the wheels to prevent free flight until he accumulated sufficient practise in controlling the machine. However, on 31 July the last run ended in considerable damage because one of the restraining axle trees doubled up and the lift was so great that the upper track was broken, liberating the machine which floated through the air for some 600 ft before sinking into the soft turf. 'It was the first time in the world that a powered flying machine had actually lifted itself and its crew into the air,' Maxim jubilantly declared.

He had his critics. On 25 August Frederick Stringfellow received a letter from Thomas Moy writing from his Office for Patents in Chancery Lane: 'Maxim's boasting has raised a silly hubbub about aerial navigation, and there is nothing practical in all that has been printed. Maxim's machine is a bad copy of Henson's, lately altered to tally somewhat with your father's 1868 machine. I have written to Mr Chanute in Chicago that I would give Maxim fifty years and he would not accomplish aë.nav[n]. I agree with you entirely as to Phillip's Venetian blind.'

That last reference was to Horatio Phillips' impracticable flying machine composed of fifty narrow, lath-like 19-foot winglets set one above the other two inches apart.

Moy's next paragraphs indicate that Frederick was still experimenting with steam engines, for he continues: 'I have enquired about steam gauges. Mr Buck has some very neat, 1 inch diameter, registering up to 80 lbs. You must bear in mind with small models that any leak at high pressure is much worse than a leak at a lower pressure. In consequence of this we sometimes get more power at 60 lbs than we do at 150. The price of these little gauges is 12s.' He adds a postscript, 'I have presented your book to the Patent Office Library. I have read it through with very great interest.'

Probably at that time Fred Stringfellow was experiencing one of his recurrent shortages of money and sought to cash in on his father's redundant effects, for on 14 October 1895 he wrote to another Aeronautical member, G Crosland Taylor: 'In the early forties my late father constructed a boiler of the same (cone) type for a common road Steam Carriage. It is made of copper, seven cones about 4½ inches diameter at top end and about 20 inches long. Contained in an iron case with fireplace and complete, it

weighed about 40 lbs. The measurement is about 2 ft 9½ inches at
the top of the dome and width about 13 inches. Will stand a
pressure of about 300 lbs. I have the boiler now and would be glad
to sell it cheap.' However, action was slow to follow.

*   *   *

In the following year that mainstay of the Aeronautical Society
and intimate friend of the Stringfellows, Frederick W Brearey
died, and Major B F S Baden-Powell became Secretary.
Concurrently came rumours from the USA of Professor Langley's
achievement in obtaining successful flights with a steam-
powered, tandem-wing model weighing 28 lbs and spanning 14 ft.
Unlike John Stringfellow with his model of two decades earlier
or Frederick John's model biplane and current quintuplane,
Langley's trials were recorded by an indisputable witness — Dr
Graham Bell, inventor of the telephone, who said, 'Two flights
were made in such manner that no one could fail to recognise that
the practicability of mechanical flight had been demonstrated.'

In more expansive terms than the modest John Stringfellow
had ever used, Langley stated: 'I have brought to a close a
portion of the work which seemed to be specially mine — the
demonstration of the practicability of mechanical flight; and for
the next stage, which is the commercial and practical development of the idea, it is probable that the world may look to others.
The world indeed will be supine if it does not realise that a new
possibility has come to it, and that the great universal highway
overhead is now soon to be opened.' However, that task was still
to take several more years, during which many others contributed
their quota, and success would only be achieved by using the
relatively light internal combustion petrol engine used at that time
to drive the earliest automobiles, of which the first to take the
road had been a Panhard-Levassor in 1891.

Meanwhile emphasis was still on Fred's steam engines, with
Crosland Taylor writing to the Australian aviation enthusiast
Lawrence Hargrave on 12 December 1896, telling him: 'I went
about four weeks ago to see F. J. Stringfellow at Crewkerne (I
dare say you have his pamphlet on Flying machines) to see his
cone boiler. It is made of cones about the following proportions,
which are connected up top and bottom to a receiver, and 3 sq ft
are supposed to equal 1 hp and will get up 100 lbs of steam in 4
minutes or even less. I was told 2½ minutes. However, it is to
come to our works to test for the purpose of a motor car. It was
made forty years ago and is all thin copper and contains 6 sq ft
heated surface . . .'

But Taylor forgot to complete and post the letter and ultimately wrote to Hargrave on 27 April of the following year: 'I have just found this letter to you in my works desk. Thought I had sent it and I must have been interrupted and forgot it, however. The above boiler contains nearly 7 sq ft of surface and weighs 15 lbs and is 16 inches high, 17 inches long and 5 inches wide, 28 cones and a receiver on top. I am going to make a boiler like it only stronger and larger for a motor car which will have four cylinders direct onto the wheels.'

Visits and letters continued to be exchanged between Alderson and Fred Stringfellow. The next letter to survive was that of 11 May 1897 from Fred who wrote: 'I was delighted to get your letter as I was afraid I had wearied you with my continual croaking as to my health. As the doctor said, it is not going to kill me but it is most awfully unpleasant having to suffer so and this morning I have had an extra amount of suffering (but the moral is I may be better this afternoon). As you say, work early and late wears one out, and all the summer I have been up from 4 or 5 am to complete my last model, but now I feel quite done up as the dental business for the last month has been a rush, for which from a pecuniary sense I have been grateful although I would rather have it steady.

'The gladioli have been a treat to me as I am rather partial to good things! I have enclosed a list of those you kindly presented to me with remarks. As to your kind offer of the yellow Arum Lily, if it requires heat I should have to get a friend to start it but I do not see why after a time it should not do as well as the common white.

'I have been unable to try any experiments with my last apparatus as I have to attend to business, but trust you will be successful in your trials (of your flying models). Of course I have seen the accounts of Langley's experiments, but remember that in 1847 the many trials my late father had before he could liberate the machine in the air. The repeated trials to obtain the correct balance almost seemed wearisome at the time, but at last was crowned with success in 1848 — and so it is with anything like a mechanical contrivance for artificial flight. I must say in 1847 my father succeeded in demonstrating the practicability of artificial flight that was as perfect as Langley in 1896.

'I trust you will be successful with your battery, and your experiments be all you wish. I have not seen the Aeronautical Annual, but as to Chanute's and Herring's experiments in gliding, I can imagine what they are after reading the early experiments of Sir George Cayley, and it does not appear so very much advancement has been made as we have a right to expect.'

Frederick Stringfellow, now aged sixty-four, kept his models with those of his father's and the steam engine relics in a shed at the bottom of the garden at Candle Cottage. Apparently either remnants of his father's rumoured full-size machine or much of the original big 20 ft model had survived, for Walter Clark, a friend of Fred's fifth son Vernon B T Stringfellow, remembered: 'The old plane was parked down at the cottage and we lads used to have a rare old time playing with it.'

Vernon had attended Crewkerne Grammar School and he and Clark used to play for St Michael's Guild Rugby Club, but now he was being trained as a dentist by his father. He liked playing pranks in company with his photographer brothers who had a photographic studio and a dark room at the bottom of the garden. Their father found it a place of quiet retreat, and after seeing him go there one day the boys crept silently down and saw he was fast asleep with his mouth wide open. Quietly they took his photograph, developed and printed it, then put it on the newspaper on his lap so that on awakening he would see how awful he looked!

*   *   *

The years rolled on. Gladstone had died in 1898, and the Sudan war had been in the background from 1896 to 1899, but following Sir Herbert Kitchener's victory at Omdurman the Valley of the Nile was placed under the 'sphere of British influence'.

Fred Stringfellow continued to maintain his interest in aviation, though his garden seems to have had priority. On 11 July 1899 he wrote to Alderson: 'I must thank you for the fine plant of yellow or sulphur Carnation you kindly sent. I ought to have done so before but have been very dicky latterly, otherwise I should have run up to London last Saturday week and stayed until Monday evening as I had a chance of doing so for 5s. However, if I do feel well enough I shall certainly contrive to spend a few days in town this summer.

'By the by, you did not give me any name to the Carnation you sent me. My little garden is as usual this year. Cactus dahlias, of which I have several in full bloom such as Starfish, Cycle, Beatrice, James Basham, Miss Webster etc. etc. I have a splendid bed of ten week Calcelerias etc., etc., and then on the Court I have close upon two hundred pots of flowers, but my Begonias are very backward — still the place looks gaily bright.

'I trust you are prospering and all are well. I shall be at Seaton on Thursday. I wish you were with me, but I assure you I cannot walk about much as the least fatigue brings on the horrible pains in my chest. I began this letter early this morning but have been interrupted so often that I was afraid I should not have time to finish today.

'Have you heard anything of how friend Moy succeeded with

his new apparatus? I am afraid he did not find it so good as he anticipated or he surely would have written to tell me.

'I shall begin some fresh (flying) experiments I trust tomorrow. I fancy it singular nothing further has been done than Father did in 1848. That is, make a machine with screw propelled planes fly. Certainly Maxim's experiments were not a success, but Professor Langley made one fly in 1897, though I cannot tell by the photograph whether it was gradually descending or if at any time it flew higher than the point of departure. In my Father's experiments the machine was always on the rise. It seems unfortunate that nothing but small models up to the present time have flown. Still I believe the principle to be correct and when we get a lighter and more powerful engine the matter will be easily accomplished. As to Chanute's experiments, I do not think much of them.'

Frederick Stringfellow's letters make no mention of current affairs, but scarcely had the Sudan war ceased than the Boer War began, following President Kruger's refusal to give the influx of English and other gold seeking 'Uitlanders' the same civil rights and privileges as the Transvaal citizens, and he asserted the complete independence of that country. On 9 October 1899 the Transvaal Executive forwarded the ultimatum to the British Government demanding withdrawal of British troops, and stating that if the terms were not accepted within forty-eight hours the refusal of her Majesty's Government would be considered a declaration of war. The British replied that the demand was impossible to discuss. Immediately the Transvaal Boers invaded Natal and the sad years of sporadic war began. Soon enormous reinforcements were sent to the Cape from England and the Supreme Command was entrusted to Lord Roberts, with Kitchener as Chief of Staff.

In the last weeks of 1899 Britain had suffered a series of defeats, but by February 1900 the tide turned. The towns of Ladysmith and Kimberley were relieved and in May Mafeking was freed. What a time of revelry and wild rejoicing there was that night in London! Colonel Baden-Powell (brother of the Aeronautical Society's Secretary) who had been commander of the besieged town, became a national hero. Pretoria was captured by Lord Roberts the following month; whereupon President Kruger fled to Europe, but though that meant the Boers had no chance of securing victory they continued a long guerilla campaign against Kitchener's troops. In June there was also serious trouble in China where a fanatical sect called the 'Boxers' rose in rebellion, and in August a large international European army had to be despatched to relieve the European legation and quell the rising. Meanwhile the war in South Africa ground on.

Chapter 12
An End and a Beginning

Opening his morning paper on 23 January 1901 Fred Stringfellow found that on the previous day 'our Great and beloved Queen passed away at Osborne Palace in the 82nd year of her age after a reign of 64 years, the longest and most beneficial in the annals of our history'. Certainly Britain had become the most powerful nation in the world with a far-flung Empire which now included the Commonwealth of Australia by the Queen's Proclamation of the previous September.

The turn of the century marked a very different world from John Stringfellow's day. Long-distance travel which had once involved great sailing ships now used huge steamers such as the *Kaiser William* of 14,000 tons which had just secured the Blue Riband of the Atlantic with a crossing of under six days. On land there were extensive railway systems in every country, with express trains travelling at the fearsome speed of 60 mph, though on the roads horse traffic still reigned supreme despite the incursion of a few new-fangled automobiles driven by petrol engines, which to the dismay of the countryside were permitted to travel at 20 mph!

The accession of Edward VII found Britain still at war in South Africa, but trade and industry had grown by leaps and bounds, and with it a new middle class in society with high ideals and strict morality, yet with greater freedoms than ever before, including an annual holiday by the seaside and engagement in wide-ranging sports. Even the emancipation of women had become a creed, attracting such active workers as that same Margaret Bondfield whose father had helped John Stringfellow with his bird collection and early experiments with hand launched model gliders. One day she was to become the first women Cabinet Minister.

Significantly, not only was the first British submarine launched in 1901 but also the first of the imposing Zeppelin rigid airships in Germany. Nevertheless the older generation still asserted that 'If the Almighty had meant men to fly he would have fitted them with wings'. Yet already, a number of experimenters had been successful in briefly sailing the air with hang gliders, though in Germany, the world's greatest exponent, Otto Lilienthal, had been killed and shortly afterwards Percy Pilcher encountered similar disaster in England.

Maxim had dropped the idea of powered flight for the time being, but his Vickers/Maxim company had followed up a similar idea to John Stringfellow's 1879 patent for his wheeled 'apparatus for affording protection from bullets and other missiles' by producing a motor-driven 'travelling fort' comprising an armoured lozenge-shaped vehicle carrying a dozen soldiers and their guns, which was demonstrated at motor cycle trials held at the Crystal Palace in April 1902. However, no ordered followed, and in the following month a Peace Treaty was at last signed with the Boers at Pretoria. For his services in the South African guerilla war Kitchener was made a Viscount and awarded the Order or Merit.

*   *   *

At the beginning of 1903 Alderson urged Frederick Stringfellow to participate in an Aeronautical Exhibition which was to be held at the Alexandra Palace in March that year, and on 1 February Stringfellow wrote in reply to several matters: 'I think an apology is due from me in not answering your letter earlier. In the first place do not think of sending me a Cumberland ham as I assure you I do not feel equal to accepting it.

'I am afraid Mr Moy's machine will not act as he wishes. I was sorry to hear he had been unwell, also Mr Keith, and I trust they are better. I heard from the Secretary of the Aeronautical Institute and Club thanking me for the pamphlet, and asking me certain questions as to propellers making a current of air injurious to the effective support of the planes. Now I always understood that if there was a current of 10 mph passing under the plane it was so much added to the forward speed and assisted in the support; in fact in a breeze the machine could be anchored and the wind passing under it at a certain speed would support the apparatus.

'I had a terrible mishap with my machine which was hanging in the workshop and fell down, catching the upper part of the framework and broke it to pieces — but I have put it to right again. As to sending anything to your June exhibition, I am afraid I have not much worth sending. There is part of the tail and car of the first constructed; also the wings slightly altered of the machine which flew in 1848, also the tail. The engine and boiler were given to Sir John Amery.

'I was glad to hear your description of the meeting and hear Sir Richard Barrington's praise of Maxim's machine. I think the only difficulty is to rise, but as to coming down safely, that is easy! I do not exactly agree with you as to Maxim's bent axle. I believe the machine was so tied that on coming into the air a gust of wind so twisted it as to bend the axle. Had a little more latitude been given it might not have occurred, but I know the difficulty of keeping a machine level in contrary winds until the speed is sufficient to overcome the gusty atmosphere.'

The latter statement clearly implies that he had made trials in the open air, thus confirming the hear-say.

On 15 March Fred Stringfellow wrote again: 'My dear Friend Alderson — I am sorry I was so unwell last Friday when I sent the case off to Mr W T Dunn, but I was thoroughly out of sorts and obliged to leave the packing to my son. The carpenter in the first place made the case too large and I had to have it altered, but I sent it off in time for the 4.49 passenger train Friday. The contents of the case were:- Car of large (20 ft) machine with original covering and portion of original tail. Pair large propellers, and pair small propellers which flew in 1848. Tail of same machine. Wings of planes which belonged to 1848 machine. Smaller wings or planes. Engine of 1868 machine made by my late Father. Small pair of white propellers. Small pair of red silk propellers. Lithograph of old machine. Letter announcing prize 1868. I trust the Institute of Engineers found them of service, and as I thought you may want them for your exhibition I wrote to Mr Dunn that if so to hand them to you.

'I am thankful to say I feel better and if I do not have any return of the complaint which attacked me bad last Friday I shall get on.' Apparently he was suffering from angina.

The Alexandra Palace Exhibition duly took place beneath a panoply of flags strung from gallery to gallery in the main hall. Dominating one end was a 20 ft biplane kite constructed by the cowboy-garbed, bearded Samuel Cody. Adjacent were several other large kites including a 3-winged tandem as well as various model gliders. Centrally in the other half of the hall were inflated balloons with typical wicker baskets standing for inspection on the floor. In the adjoining aisle on one side was Fred Stringfellow's quintuplane, the only powered machine there. In the opposite aisle, stacked upright, were the two half wings of his father's 1848 model and two smaller wings which could have been either his subsequent model or Frederick's biplane. On a table were the two large and two small two-bladed propellers, and nearby was the original Henson/Stringfellow cabin. Fred Stringfellow must have visited to assemble his quintuplane, but there is no reference to this in surviving correspondence.

On 5 April he wrote to Alderson: 'Many thanks for your last letter. I received the £1 from the Secretary of the Junior Engineers Institute and shall send a receipt on Tuesday as I shall be away tomorrow.

'I am sure you have been to great trouble to get the agreement back. Not that it is of any intrinsic value. You misunderstand me re my current model. I do not wish anyone to advance money, but I think it is a pity I shall be unable to try it for want of means. I should like to take it to a place and get the balance correct and try a few experiments with some fresh propellers, then if the thing will support itself, throw it off and let it do the best. But you see this would mean a little ready cash as I have to live, and if I neglect the little (dentistry) doing it would be all up with me — so you see I want a friend who has a little time at his disposal, and if there was anything to gain, of course he would have share of it. I have sent the negatives of the apparatus and you will see one is a stereo which I think will give a good idea of the large engine and boiler. By the by, I have the larger boiler which was made for a common road steam carriage. I should be glad to see it sell cheap, but it would want new casing.

'I enclose an old photo of Father, but I have not one of myself, and the Masonic one is scarcely right to expose generally, but I will see what can be done.

'In 1868 Mr Moy was scarcely friendly with us as he and Mr Shill (I believe that was his name) were trying their best to defeat us, but that was so long ago he may forget. A thought just strikes me. Mr Northcote Spicer, son of the Mr Spicer who saw the flights in 1848, is still alive and he may have heard his late father speak of it, if so his evidence would be useful as he is the only one left alive who knew anything about it except myself.'

However, Spicer's reply on 20 April was not of much value although he ascribed the so-called Henson machine to John Stringfellow's genius, saying: 'I remember hearing that the Aerial Machine that the late Mr Stringfellow invented, and with which he made experiments in flight on Bewley Down where he encamped for sometime, was the first machine of the kind that could be made to fly, but that the difficulty he had to contend with was the want of power in balancing the machine when in the air, but I understand he overcame this when he exhibited the machine at Crystal Palace and took a prize.'

On 15 August Fred wrote to Alderson explaining the method of launching his models: 'I forgot to enclose the carrier for the stretched wire for the machine, but I think you will see from the enclosed rough sketch that the manner of trying the models is very easy. You first stretch a long inclined wire and in the double end place the block for liberating the machine. By raising the jointed pieces under each end wire you can raise the front end to the required height. Then run the model on the wire and you will see the length of run the machine takes to support itself. That is

the proper length to start from, but it is useless to throw it off
before the proper balance is obtained, so I stretch a piece of
canvas on ropes under the liberating place to catch it if not right
— so you can see it is very easy to experiment with this, but I
have no time or place to experiment with.

'I hope you are well. I get on slowly but gradually improve. I
saw the Moth plant of which I sent you seed, in flower this week.
What changeable weather we are having.

'P.S. You did not say if the boiler would be of any service to
you.'

That was the last of the extant letters between the two men, but
Alderson's interest in saving the Stringfellow relics continued,
and it is unlikely that Fred Stringfellow's devotion to aeronautical
matters evaporated. He remained a member of the Aeronautical
Society and would have seen in the July issue of the Journal an
account of an International Kite Exhibition held on the Sussex
Downs, attended by over a thousand spectators, in which the
histrionic Samuel Cody was one of the competitors. Next year his
man-lifting kites were adopted by the British Army; but in the
meantime on 18 December 1903 a small paragraph in the *Daily
Mail* declared that:

> 'Messrs Wilbur and Orville Wright of Ohio yesterday
> successfully experimented with a flying machine at Kitty
> Hawk, North Carolina.'

In no way did that convey this was an epochal event in which
each of those two men in turn had briefly skimmed the sand dunes
for a few seconds with a simple power-driven home-made biplane.
Nobody would have believed it.

Oblivious of further flights by the Wrights, Major Baden-
Powell, now President of the Aeronautical Society, offered a
prize of £10 for a model weighing one pound that would fly at
least 100 yards. Nobody except Alderson seemed aware that over
half a century earlier John Stringfellow's steam model had led the
way with at least forty feet in rising flight and thus had introduced
the epoch of successful heavier-than-air-flight. But his son
Frederick John did not live to see the consequence of the new Air
Age, for he died on 25 August 1905. A typical obituary somewhat
scantily stated: 'The death of Mr F. J. Stringfellow, son of the
famous J. Stringfellow, is the breaking of yet another direct link
with the very foundation of the science of flight in this country,
for it was his father who made the first successful power-driven
model which demonstrated the phenomenon of dynamic flight for
the first time in 1848. Previously J. Stringfellow was associated
with W. S. Henson, and together they produced a model which

was not successful on trial, but is perhaps the best known of all early ideas in flying machines. F. J. Stringfellow carried on his father's work with a biplane but was unable to properly complete his experiments. Quite apart from the interest associated in the construction of models as flying machines, it is equally important to remember that the Stringfellows showed remarkable ability in making small engines, which was quite a problem in itself and has exercised the minds of many other flight pioneers. All the machinery of his father's models, Mr F. J. Stringfellow has bequeathed his youngest son, Mr V. Stringfellow.'

The technical implications were beyond the scope of journalists, and even Alderson was unaware of the full range of models which both Stringfellows had made, so *The English Mechanic* of 15 September could only say in tribute: 'After a prolonged illness Mr Fred J. Stringfellow died at his residence in Crewkerne on the 25th ult. He was the last survivor of those who witnessed the experiments conducted by his father, Mr J. Stringfellow of Chard, in 1848 with the first successful flying machine that carried and was propelled by its own motive power. This model was propelled by steam through distances varying from 20 to 40 yards, frequently rising as much as 1 in 7 during the course of its flight. The original model which flew is still in the possession of the Stringfellow family. Mr F. Stringfellow continued his father's experiments, making various machines and light steam engines; but lack of means apparently hindered advanced results.'

*   *   *

Certainly Alderson was determined that the historic success of John Stringfellow in achieving the world's first power-driven flight should be perpetuated for posterity, and to that end discussed this with 36 year-old Patrick Young Alexander, who had inherited from his father the large sum (for those days) of £60,000 which he was destined to spend on furthering aviation. He was a notable man — balloonist, safari hunter and inveterate traveller. By 1896 he had become widely known among Aeronautical Society members as an authority on the possibilities of flight; had visited Otto Lilienthal in Germany to see him gliding and had been in close touch with such British experimenters as Maxim, Moy, Wenham, Phillips and Pilcher as well as the American investigators Octave Chanute, Professor Langley and Dr A Graham Bell of telephone fame. In 1902 he had gone to America to meet Orville and Wilbur Wright after hearing from Chanute of their gliding experiments, then visited them again in January 1904, subsequently holding a meeting with the Aeronautical Society in March in which he described their pioneering power flights of the previous December. He readily undertook to buy the Stringfellow relics and present them to the nation if Alderson could make the arrangements and refurbish the models. Thereupon the latter wrote on 9 September 1905 to Eric Bruce, the contemporary Secretary of the Aeronautical Society under Baden-Powell's chairmanship: 'You will have no doubt noticed the death of Mr F. J. Stringfellow of Crewkerne recorded in the Press recently. It appears to be usual with aeronautical experimenters that he has left his family very badly provided for, and consequently they wish to realise what they can on the various machines etc. that have been made by the above and his father.

'The following are, I believe, what they refer to:-
1) Portions of the original machine made by Henson and J. Stringfellow (1843-7). This I infer was the first heavier-than-air-machine designed and constructed with a view to mechanical propulsion.
2) The original Agreement drawn up between Henson and Stringfellow in 1842.
3) Relics of the model made by J. Stringfellow 1848 which undoubtedly was the first flying machine to make successful flight.
4) A very beautifully constructed model made by the late Mr F. J. Stringfellow, which as far as I can recollect could be fitted with either a single pair of curved vanes or with two pairs superposed.
5) Light model steam engines and probably other things of interest to the aeronautical world.

'The thought that comes to my mind is that if you would be good enough to bring this communication before the President of the Society, Major Baden-Powell, and the numerous influential members of the Committee, they could place the matter before the authorities of the South Kensington Museum, and I think that the fact that the Museum at Washington U.S.A. has already acquired one of J. Stringfellow's machines, viz that shown at the Crystal Palace 1868, ought to make it a duty on the part of the Executive of our museums to secure at least the relics of 1) and 2) of the first constructed machine, 3) as the first success in mechanical propulsion, and possibly the model 4) which is really an example of skilled workmanship.

'It will thus be recorded in a definite practical manner that to England belongs the honour of being the first to successfully attempt to navigate the air. Should you approve my scheme, it would perhaps be best, being more direct, for you to communicate with Mr V. Stringfellow, a dentist of Crewkerne, Somersetshire, if you desire to ascertain any further particulars.'

The Secretary of the Aeronautical Society duly wrote, and on 28 December of that year, Valentine Stringfellow replied: 'I regret that I have not answered your letters before, but I have been away from home. You say that one of the members of the Aeronautical Society would purchase the machines. Does he want them for experimental purposes or only as curiosities? I do not ask this question idly as only one machine is complete with engine, boiler, wings etc., the other being the framework of the 1848 machine which was claimed to be the first aeroplane carrying its own motor power to rise in the air, and as such would only be useful to some museum, or as a curiosity. With regard to the former, the wings with which it is now fitted are, I believe, removeable as there are other wings for it, and also the propellers etc. Would he require these? Would he be prepared to defray the cost of cases and carriage? There is also the framework of another machine and a boiler. The sum you mention is a very low one. I would part with the machines for £25 but do not think this anything like the value of them. I should be glad if you would address your reply to 9, Kingston, Yeovil, as this will save delay as I am away from home all next week.'

In a follow-up to Bruce, Alderson had re-emphasised the proposal saying: 'I have examined at the British Museum Library the article in the *Popular Science Review* Volume vii No. xxx 1869 in which the late Mr Brearey gives in full detail the various machines, and on pages 6 and 7 gives particulars of the 1848 machine and descriptions of the successful experiments therewith. As this emanates direct from Mr Brearey there can be little doubt as to the authenticity of the claim. Some years later in 1892 the son of the inventor, Mr F. J. Stringfellow, wrote a little pamplet, but this was mainly composed of a verbatim reproduction of Mr Bearey's article.'

Unfortunately, committees take their time. There was no decision at the Society's next meeting. Queries were raised, and on 7 April 1906, Alderson re-explained the position more specifically: 'Mr Alexander has deputed me to write to you in reply to your letter of 22 March in regard to the Stringfellow relics. If you will bring the matter before the authorities of the Victoria and Albert Museum in the manner you indicate, it will be in accordance with Mr Alexander's wishes.

'The machines will be restored entirely without cost to the Aeronautical Society, but it will take some time to do this, probably by about June next if the work is not delayed by any unforseen circumstance. The following two machines will be as far as possible in their original condition as used in the Stringfellow experiments, but at present are in separate pieces and damaged, requiring much care and thought in repairing same:-

1) The Henson/Stringfellow machine, model of 1842/3. Prior to this date no machine had actually been constructed using MECHANICAL power for experimental purposes, although 'gliders' and apparatus worked by manual power had previously been built and tested. We have the hull, tail, propellers, old silk and steam engine etc. The only part to reconstruct would be the supporting area, which can be easily fixed.

2) A flying machine measuring about 10 feet tip to tip. This is the FIRST machine which actually did fly through the air and was constructed solely by J. Stringfellow after Henson left for America. The first successful flight was in 1848. This was frequently repeated before different audiences and is quite authentically recorded. I have the wings and tail here in Farnborough, the propellers and probably the hull are in Mr Alexander's care at Portsmouth, so this model can easily be re-constructed. The only thing missing is the engine.

3) There is also in the offer to the Museum an example of the peculiar form of steam-boiler adopted and exclusively used in these historic experiments.

'Further there is a complete model by Frederick Stringfellow, son of the inventor, which is a five superposed plane machine which you would probably notice at the latest Motor Exhibition in the Agricultural Hall, Islington. Should you desire more detailed information, either Mr Alexander or myself would be very pleased to furnish same. We would feel obliged if as soon as you can conveniently do so, you would inform us of the decision of the Museum authorities so that the work may proceed.'

Action ponderously followed. On 14 May the Secretary of the Board of Education wrote to Eric Bruce: 'In reply to your letter of the 5th instant, addressed to Mr Last, stating that Mr P. Y. Alexander had been so good as to offer to present to this Museum a model of the Henson-Stringfellow flying machine of 1842/3 and also one of the Stringfellow machines of 1847/8, I am directed to state that the Board would like to have these models inspected by one of Their Officers and They would be obliged if you will please state when and where they can be seen.'

In due course inspection was made and the offer of the wingless 20 foot span Henson-Stringfellow model and its engine was accepted, whereupon Alderson set about the restoration, and in mid-1907 it was presented by Patrick Alexander to the Science Museum, but without engine or the boiler which he had given to the Aeronautical Society. The re-built model undoubtedly closely followed the original patented design, though Stringfellow may not have had it in precisely that form. There were minor errors such as the undercarriage tricycle which was slightly different and too narrow for lateral support, the bracing pylons too long, and the vital stabilising top fin was not fitted. The propellers were assumed to be two-bladers, presumably based on the very large example revealed centrally in the studio photograph of the Bat model, though the Patent specification drawings show six-bladers.

Alderson did not attempt to rebuild the successful 1847/8 Stringfellow model, but presented the component relics to the Museum the following year (1908). However they were in such poor condition that the Museum craftsmen decided re-construction was not feasible — the wing camber, for instance, had lost all its curvature, leaving a more abrupt step at the rear spar juncture of the flexible trailing edge than is apparent in the studio photographs. Nearly twenty years later, M J B Davy, when Keeper of the Museum, took the deteriorated components as a guide and had a reproduction built which, despite a guess at the bracing and wing section, must be a close approximation of the original, and like the earlier 'Aerial Carriage' is a remarkable forecast of the shape and structure of the man-carrying aeroplanes that evolved more than fifty years later. What is now wanted as confirmation of those early trials is a contemporary model to test in free air, for it undoubtedly could fly for several miles if the air was calm, and if moveable controls were added it should perform under radio control like any modern model.

For me, the long arm of coincidence plays a part in the story because in 1925 I joined the small Westland Aircraft Works subsidiary of Petters Ltd, the then world-famous oil-engine manufacturers of Yeovil, fifteen miles from Chard, and came to know Benjamin Joseph Jacobs, the retired chief designer of the engine business — a tall, grizzled man with steel-rimmed spectacles, who was often to be seen sedately cycling to his old love, the nearby Petter engine factory. When in 1893 one of the twin brother founders of that firm, Percival Waddons Petter was the manager of his father's foundry and engineering works, 33 year-old Jacobs had been his foreman.

Percy Petter told me: 'Mr Jacobs and I often in the nineties discussed the possibility of designing an aeroplane with a light internal-combustion engine, especially after, through his introduction, I had the pleasure of meeting Mr Stringfellow and seeing his models.'

He meant Frederick John Stringfellow, but Jacobs had known

178 An Ancient Air

all the Stringfellow family and so was able to describe John Stringfellow to me as: 'A wonderful man of great talent who showed Henson how to make an aeroplane fly but took no credit, for he shunned publicity and always went his own quiet way.'

On a plaque in the Queen Victoria Jubilee Council Chamber of Chard Town Hall, and again on the house where Stringfellow lived at the top of High Street, he is proudly described as 'Inventor of the Aeroplane', but his imposing memorial grave states more accurately: 'Inventor of the first engine driven aeroplane'.

Though he was the epoch-making introducer of successful powered flight, John Stringfellow had no illusion that it was more than a beginning, for he modestly told the Aeronautical Society of Great Britain: 'Somebody must do better than I have done with the wing before we succeed with Aerial Navigation.'

His son Frederick John urged that same endeavour: 'It may be to many an ancient dream, but science has shown it is more than possible, and science never stands still. Objectors may quibble, for they have done so in all ages, and if they had been listened to by the apparent dreaming searchers after great ends, we should now have been without what we esteem the necessaries of civilization. Let our motto be "onwards and upwards" to win another triumph over nature; to make use of that highway above us; to show that man is indeed the Creator's most perfect handiwork; to assert the dominion given to us by working out many inventions to lead to this great triumph over the difficulties of space and time.'

Index